The Story of the Cambrian

A Biography of

C. P. Gasquoine

Alpha Editions

This edition published in 2024

ISBN : 9789362997814

Design and Setting By
Alpha Editions
www.alphaedis.com
Email - info@alphaedis.com

As per information held with us this book is in Public Domain.
This book is a reproduction of an important historical work. Alpha Editions uses the best technology to reproduce historical work in the same manner it was first published to preserve its original nature. Any marks or number seen are left intentionally to preserve its true form.

Contents

PREFACE. ....- 1 -

CHAPTER I. BIRTH AND PARENTAGE.............................- 3 -

CHAPTER II. A BIRTHDAY PARTY. ....- 14 -

CHAPTER III. EARLY
DEVELOPMENTS AND DIFFICULTIES.............................- 21 -

THE CEREMONY. ....- 29 -

CHAPTER IV. OSWESTRY TO
NEWTOWN. ....- 31 -

CHAPTER V. FROM THE SEVERN TO
THE SEA. ....- 41 -

CHAPTER VI. THE BATTLE OF
ELLESMERE. ....- 52 -

CHAPTER VII. THE COAST SECTION. ....- 60 -

CHAPTER VIII. SOME EARLIER
BRANCHES. ....- 68 -

CHAPTER IX. CONSOLIDATION. ....- 76 -

CHAPTER X. INCIDENTS AND ACCIDENTS. ....- 83 -

CHAPTER XI. THE CAMBRIAN OF TO-DAY. ....- 97 -

APPENDIX. ....- 108 -

PREFACE.

Credit for the inspiration of this book belongs to my friend, Mr. W. R. Hall, of Aberystwyth, who, in one of his interesting series of "Reminiscences" of half a century of Welsh journalism, contributed to the "Cambrian News," recently expressed his surprise that no one had hitherto attempted to write the history of the Cambrian Railways. With the termination of that Company's separate existence, on its amalgamation with the Great Western Railway under the Government's grouping scheme, "the hour" for such an effort seems to have struck; and Mr. Hall's pointed indication of Oswestry as the most appropriate place where the work could be undertaken, not only by reason of its close connection with the official headquarters of the Cambrian, but because, in a certain newspaper office there lay the files containing so many old records of the railway's birth and early struggles for existence, even the selection of "the man" appeared so severely circumscribed that to the present writer it virtually amounted to what, in certain ecclesiastical circles, is termed "a call."Responsibility for its acceptance, however, and for the execution of the task, with its manifold imperfections and shortcomings, rests entirely with the author, whose only qualification for assuming the rôle of biographer of the Cambrian is the deep interest he has always taken in a subject worthy of a far abler pen. Not even the attempt would have been possiblehad it not been for the valuable assistance readily given by many kind friends directly or indirectly associated with the Cambrian Railways.Special thanks are due, and hereby gratefully acknowledged, to Mr. Samuel Williamson General Manager, not for only much personal trouble taken in supplying information and looking through proof-sheets, but for placing no small portion of the time of some members of his clerical staff at the disposal of the author, who has troubled them on many occasions, but never without receiving prompt and patient response; to other officials and employees, past and present, of the Company for information regarding their several departments, and their personal recollections, including Mr. T. S. Goldsworthy, the senior officer and sole surviving member of the "old guard," who played their part in the battles of the Parliamentary Committee-rooms of long ago, whose reminiscences of the days of old have proved particularly useful; to the Earl of Powis for permission to inspect the voluminous papers of the late Earl, whose name was so intimately associated with the early development of railway schemes in Montgomeryshire; to the family of the late Mr. David Howell for similar facilities in regard to his papers; and, for the loan of photographs or assistance of varied sort to Colonel Apperley, Mr. E. D. Nicholson, Park Issa, Oswestry, Mr. W. P. Rowlands and Mr. Edmund Gillart, Machynlleth, Mr. Robert Owen, Broad Street, Welshpool, Mr. J.

Harold Thomas, Garth Derwen, Buttington, the Misses Ward, Whittington, Miss Mickleburgh, Oswestry, Mr. E. Shone, Oswestry, the Editor of the "Peterborough Advertiser," the publishers of the "Great Western Magazine," and others. The indexing has been compiled by Mr. Kay, Public Librarian, Oswestry, to whom thanks are due for the efficient discharge of a rather irksome duty. As to the arrangement of the book itself: in tracing the various stages of construction, often simultaneous or overlapping in point of time, of the several separate and formerly independent undertakings into which the Cambrian system was subsequently consolidated, and still further augmented by later local amalgamations, it has been found well-nigh impossible, chronologically, to maintain at once a clear and consecutive story. Recourse has, therefore, been had to the method of dealing with each section of the line in separate chapters, and the same plan applies to some departments of development in later years. But an endeavour has been made to follow, as comprehensively as such circumstances permit, the general course of the Railway's growth; and it is in the hope that, however imperfectly, it may serve to recal seventy years of struggle, triumph and romance in Welsh railway annals that to Lt.-Col. David Davies, M.P., its last Chairman, and Mr. Samuel Williamson, its last General Manager, and his numerous other friends among the officers and staff of all ranks, the writer begs to dedicate this little story of the Cambrian, in memory of many happy days spent in travelling, as a privileged passenger, along its far-reaching lines.

C. P. G.

"Border Counties Advertizer" Office, Oswestry, 1922.

CHAPTER I. BIRTH AND PARENTAGE.

"No Engineer could succeed without having men about him as highly gifted as himself."—ROBERT STEPHENSON.

I.

When what eventually became the Cambrian Railways was born it was a very tiny baby. Compared with its ultimate frame, it possessed neither arms nor legs, nor even head, and consisted merely of heart and a small part of its trunk. It began "in the air" at Newtown and ended, if possible, in still more ethereal poise, at Llanidloes. Physical junction with existing lines there was none, and the engines—four in number—which drew the coaches that composed those early trains had to be brought by road, from Oswestry, in specially constructed wagons, not without difficulties and adventures, and placed on the metals at the railhead, to live their life and perform their duty in "splendid isolation." It was only gradually that limb after limb was added, and subsequently constructed railways were incorporated or absorbed, until the consolidated system obtained the rather attenuated proportions with which we are familiar to-day, stretching from Whitchurch, on the Cheshire border, to Aberystwyth, on the shores of Cardigan Bay, with its two chief subsidiary "sections," one (including some half dozen miles of the original track) from Moat Lane Junction to Brecon, and another from Dovey Junction to Pwllheli; shorter branches or connecting lines from Ellesmere to Wrexham, Oswestry to Llangynog, Llanymynech to Llanfyllin, Abermule to Kerry, Cemmes Road to Dinas Mawddwy, Barmouth Junction to Dolgelley, and two lengths of narrow gauge line, from Welshpool to Llanfair Caereinion and Aberystwyth to Devil's Bridge, altogether exactly 300 miles.

Such, in briefest outline, denotes how "the Cambrian" began and what it has grown to be; but there is little virtue in a mere recital of statistics, and the writing of "history," of the kind once defined by the late Lord Halsbury as "only a string of names and dates" would be no congenial task to the present author. Nor, happily, is it necessary to confine oneself to such barren and unemotional limits. It is not in the record of train miles run, of the number of passengers and the weight of the merchandise carried, or even in the dividends earned, or not earned (though these factors are not without their value to the proprietors) that the chief interest in the story of a railway lies. [2] Very often it is the tale of unending trial and difficulty and even apparent failure which holds for the spectator the largest measure of romance, and such is certainly the case of what, at one time, was, with quite as much sympathetic affection as contempt, popularly called "the poor old Cambrian." There were times when the difficulties which faced its constructors appeared to be absolutely insuperable. What with the enormous weight of its cradle, measured in gold, and the continual quarrels of its nurses, the undertaking was well nigh strangled at birth. Even when the line was actually opened for traffic a burden of financial difficulty rested upon Directors and Managers that might have crushed the spirit out of many a stout heart.

Judged by the maturer experience of long years, it is wonderful to think that, even under the most careful management, the Company should have been able to survive its constant buffetings at the hand of Fate, but survive it has, and by eternal patience and unfailing perseverance these many troubles were at length overcome, and if to-day the railway offers facilities and comforts to the travelling public that stand the test of comparison with such as are provided by the great trunk lines of England and Scotland, it is no small tribute to those who have worked long and labouring to bring its services to their present high standard of efficiency.

But of the Cambrian as we know it to-day there will be something more to be said presently. Biography, by time-honoured custom, if not necessity, begins with birth and parentage; and, though corporate bodies may often experience some difficulty about laying claim to a "lang pedigree," even a railway company cannot come into existence without considerable pre-natal labour.

Among its parents the Cambrian possessed some men of rare grit and determination. Prominent among them was one who ranks high among the makers of modern Wales, whose name has become a household word not only in his native land, but wherever Welshmen congregate throughout the world, and is still, by happy coincidence, intimately associated, in the third generation, with the Cambrian to-day. The story of David Davies of Llandinam has been fully told in other pages, [4] but it is so closely woven around the romance of the railway which he did so much to bring into being that no record of that undertaking would be complete without some reference to it, however brief. Born at a small holding called Draintewion, perched on the hillside overlooking the Severn Vale near Llandinam, the eldest of a family of nine children, on December 18, 1818,—"three eighteens," as he used in later life jocularly to remark—his boyhood was spent on the little plot of land tilling its rich soil, or helping his father, in the work of sawing timber into planks, a commodity for which public demand was then rapidly increasing. His only schooling was received in a little seminary carried on in the village church, and that wonderful educational institution of rural Wales, the Sunday School. But at the age of eleven the desk was deserted for the saw bench, and the rest of his instruction was derived at "the University of Observation, in which he took not a mere 'pass' but very high 'honours'." A keen observation of human nature, a shrewd judgment of men and beast, and a ready aptitude for application of native wit to the problems of life developed David Davies into the man of wealth and power he ultimately became. Even in his school days, however, these latent traits were not unobservable. It is recorded that "he was the winner of every game." He may have had a generous portion of what men call "luck," but to it was added the still more valuable element of industry and perseverance and healthy ambition. He knew how to take the chances which came his way, which is probably the secret of success with many who "get on." When opportunity offered to enter a new path he readily seized it, and from the hewer of wood he became the modest contractor, and ultimately the greater builder of bridges, docks and railways.

Some Parents of the Cambrian.

Passengers travelling along the Cambrian line from Moat Lane Junction to Llanidloes, may notice, at Llandinam, the roadway which runs below the church, and crosses the river on an embankment to the station. The construction of that highway was the first contract which David Davies held, and it stands to-day, hard by the statue of him which has since been erected, as a monument of his self-reliant zeal and sound workmanship. Other contracts followed, including that for the construction of Oswestry Smithfield, and it was during one of his visits to that town that Mr. Davies formed a friendship which led to a partnership that, in its turn, played a potent part in the making of the Cambrian.

For in Oswestry there lived Mr. Thomas Savin, who had been born, in 1826, at Llwynymaen, and was a partner in a mercer's business with Mr. Edward Morris (who afterwards purchased and sold the Van Mine near Caersws), under the style of Messrs. Morris and Savin. Mr. Savin's mind, however, was not entirely concentrated on measuring cloth and calico. He took a keen interest in the life of the town, and was an energetic supporter of local institutions. Elected to the Town Council in 1856, he was mayor in 1863, and appointed alderman in 1871, an office he retained to the end of his varied life. But these honours had yet to come. Already, at the time of which we are now writing, Mr. Savin had visions of a larger enterprise beyond the boundaries of his native borough.

Like many large and generous-hearted men, Mr. Savin was very impetuous and impatient of delays. On one occasion, it is related, when still a mercer at Oswestry, he drove over to a Welsh border market town to sell his wares. It was the custom there for farmers to decline to look at any other business till the sale of the live stock was disposed of, and the market being loth to start and Mr. Savin eager to be home again, he rushed into the arena and startled the company present by buying a thousand sheep. This was before he became associated with railway pioneering, but it is a characteristic example of that dramatic impulsiveness which led to his subsequent success—and failure.

Caught by the spirit of venture and enthusiasm, which had swept over the country after the successful opening of the Manchester and Liverpool Railway in 1830, his thoughts had begun to turn to railway production, and the meeting with the young Montgomeryshire road and bridge builder opened the looked for door. In a room over the tobacconist shop now occupied by Mr. Richards, opposite the Post Office, in Church Street, Oswestry, and close to the premises in which, some fifteen or sixteen years earlier another notable man, Shirley Brooks, afterwards editor of "Punch," had toiled as a lawyer's article pupil to his uncle, Mr. Charles Sabine, Mr. Davies and Mr. Savin were brought together by Mr. George Owen, himself destined to play no small part in the planning of the Cambrian. A man of Kent, native of Tunbridge Wells, Mr. Owen had begun his business career in the office of Mr. Charles Mickleburgh, land surveyor, agent and enclosure commissioner, of Montgomery, one of whose daughters he subsequently married. He worked side by side with another young engineer, of whom we shall hear more presently,—Mr. Benjamin Piercy, under whose initial leadership, Mr. Owen, as resident engineer, was to serve the local railway for many a long year. Nor was that the only capacity in which his gifts were displayed. Making Oswestry his home, he became a member of the Town Council in 1860, mayor in 1864 and 1865, and alderman in 1874. For twenty years he was a member of the General

Purposes Committee, served as borough and county magistrate, and was a member of the School Board from its inception, and chairman from 1891 till his death in 1901. Indeed, there was no interest in the town,—administrative, commercial and recreative,—in which he did not fill a conspicuous role. But, perhaps, of all his services to the community, none was more opportune or more prolific of far-reaching results than that happy inspiration of introducing Messrs. Davies and Savin.

II.

Still, it takes more than a couple of contractors, however enthusiastic, to construct a railway. Though the more visible, the organiser of the labour is not the only parent. Not less essential, in his creative function, is the capitalist; and even the powerful combination of capitalist and contractor is insufficient to carry matters to a practical conclusion without the expert guidance of the engineer. Nevertheless, Messrs. Davies and Savin, as the new partnership was termed, had not long to wait before their opportunity arrived.

The great "railway mania" which reached its climax on that notable Sunday, November 30th, 1845, to be followed by the catastrophic bursting of the bubble, had left men rather sobered in their outlook upon the future possibilities of speculation in this alluring direction. It had witnessed the formulation of no fewer than 1,263 separate railway schemes, involving an (hypothetical) expenditure of 560 millions sterling, of which 643 got no further than the issue of a prospectus, while over 500 went through all the necessary stages of being brought before Parliament and 272 actually became Acts—"to the ruin of thousands who had afterwards to find the money to fulfil the engagements into which they had so rashly entered."

Amongst these was a Bill for converting the Montgomeryshire Canal into a railway line, for which an Act was passed in 1846, but it was a hare-brained scheme and soon came to nought. Other proposals, however, developed into what promised, and have since proved, to be highly profitable enterprises. The western Midlands and North Wales had been linked by the line from Shrewsbury to Chester, which Mr. Henry Robertson, M.P., for the former town and afterwards for the County of Merioneth, in which his residence, Palé, near Corwen, was situate, had carried over the great viaducts of Chirk and Cefn. From Chester, Mr. Robert Stephenson, even more daring, had flung his extension of the North Western system, by way of

> "The magic Bridge of Bangor
> Hung awful in the sky." [8]

across the Menai Straits into Anglesey and so to Holyhead. The air was again thick, and to become thicker, with new adventures. Hardly a valley in North or Central Wales but had its ardent advocates of connecting lines. Within a short time newspaper columns were to be flooded with prospectuses of all sorts of schemes. Parliamentary committee rooms buzzed with forensic eloquence about the advantages and disadvantages of this or that route. Expert witnesses swore this, that, or anything else, as expert witnesses generally will, provided, that like the gentlemen who question and cross-question them, they are sufficiently briefed. In vain did the secluded Lake Poet protest:

> "Is there no nook of English ground secure
> From rash assault?"

The iron road was to come, and come it did, all conquering and, not so unbeneficial, after all, in its rule.

Amidst this welter of proposals and counter-proposals there emerged, sometime during 1852 a scheme, propounded by Mr. Bethell, of Westminster for constructing a railway connecting the existing line at Shrewsbury with Aberystwyth. It was to run by way of the Rea Valley, through Minsterley, and to strike the Severn Valley again in the neighbourhood of Montgomery, whence it was to continue through Newtown and Llanidloes. This was quickly followed by another for a line from Oswestry to Newtown, which was projected under Shrewsbury and Chester Railway auspices. To the latter Mr. Bethell replied by transferring his scheme to the North Western Company, whose engineers remodelled it. With a view to driving any rival Montgomeryshire scheme out of the field, the proposed new line was diverted from the Rea Valley to pass by way of Criggion and Welshpool to Newtown, with a branch from Criggion to Oswestry, and between Newtown and Aberystwyth it was altered to go by Machynlleth, instead of Llanidloes.

This sort of strategy, however, only seemed to stimulate the men of Montgomeryshire to fresh determination to show their independence, and in this they had the adventitious aid of a very influential neighbour, Mr. George Hammond Whalley.

Mr. Whalley was a very remarkable man. A native of Gloucester, according to "Debrett," he was a lineal descendant of Edward Whalley (first cousin to Oliver Cromwell and John Hampden), who signed the warrant for the execution of Charles I. At the University College, London, he carried off first prize in rhetoric and logic, afterwards was called to the bar, for some years went the Oxford Circuit and acted as Assistant Tithe Commissioner, and Examiner of Private Bills for Parliament. He lived at Plas Madoc, Ruabon, was a deputy lieutenant for Denbighshire and a magistrate for that county, Montgomeryshire and Merionethshire. In 1853 he acted as High Sheriff of Carnarvonshire, and at the time of the Crimean War he volunteered the services of the troop of Denbighshire Yeomanry Cavalry of which he was Captain and received the thanks of the War Office. Some years earlier, during the Irish famine, he established fisheries on the west coast of Ireland, and, in his own yacht, explored and ascertained the position of the fishing banks. The electors of Leominster declined to return him to Parliament in 1845, as did also the Montgomery Boroughs in 1852; but later that year he was elected for Peterborough, unseated on petition, re-elected the next year and again unseated. He unsuccessfully contested the same constituency in 1857, but was elected in May 1859 and sat till his death in 1878, during his Parliamentary career devoting a good deal of attention to the reform of private bill procedure on which he carried a not unimportant measure. But he was no mere meticulous lawyer. His frantic espousal of the Protestant cause, supposed by the timid in the middle of last century to be in some danger in England, earned him a good deal of notoriety and a popular name. Hardly more eccentric was the warm support he gave to the cause of Arthur Orton in his claim to the title and estate of Sir Roger Tichborne. On one of the last visits he paid to Oswestry he called to see a friend. As he was leaving his friend's office he suddenly turned round and asked "Do you believe in the Claimant?" The reply was an emphatic negative. "Ah," exclaimed the departing visitor, "you will come to!"

But if Mr. Whalley was a bad prophet in this respect, his instinct did not always mislead him. He believed in himself, which was not only a more substantial faith, but more to the point in this narrative, for it enabled him, by dint of self-assurance, largely to dominate, and occasionally to domineer, the railway world of Montgomeryshire and the adjacent counties and to contribute in no small measure to the successful accomplishment of several local schemes.

Conspicuous among them was the Llanidloes and Newtown. Though an isolated link in itself, it was intended to form part of a chain that was to stretch from Manchester and the industrial north to Milford Haven, a famous Welsh seaport, and this dream was constantly in the mind of local promoters whenever and wherever such sectional schemes were discussed. On October 30th, 1852, a meeting was held at Llanidloes, with Mr. Whalley in the chair, at which the project was cordially adopted, a committee formed to further its achievement by raising the necessary subscriptions, and arrangements made for carrying the fiery cross of propaganda to Newtown and Rhayader, and as far afield as Aberystwyth. On this effective errand Mr. Whalley and his coadjutors stumped the countryside, and "inn bills" began to form no inconsiderable item in the promoters' balance sheets. But nothing can be accomplished in this world without effort and expenditure; and to the missionaries' warning words against "the evil of conceding to an overbearing leviathan neighbour any privileges calculated to endanger the independence of their little company," we are informed by a chronicler of the day, "the county nobly responded, and petitions were sent from every district, praying for the recognition by Parliament of the principles so ably enunciated by Mr. Whalley."

The "little company" had, indeed, good reason to be apprehensive; but fortune favoured its course. Before this onslaught, even the "overbearing leviathan" quailed. After long and costly struggle in the Parliamentary committee rooms, accommodation was reached, and in the House of Commons the Montgomeryshire promoters' scheme passed with flying colours; but an unfortunate error, by which the levels were proved to be some 18 feet below the Severn water, wrecked it in the Lords. In August, 1853, however, the scheme received Parliamentary sanction, and out of the long list of "provisional directors" appointed the previous year, the first board was formed. They were:—Mr. Whalley, chairman; Mr. W. Lefeaux, vice-chairman; Alderman E. Cleaton, Llanidloes; Alderman Richard Holmes, Llanidloes; Mr. Wm. Lloyd, Newtown; Mr. Edward Morris, Oxon, Shrewsbury; Mr. T. E. Marsh, Llanidloes, and Mr. T. Prickard, Dderw, Radnorshire. Mr. Rice Hopkins was the engineer, Mr. T. P. Prichard, general manager, and Mr. John Jenkins, secretary. Mr. Jenkins, however, soon transferred his services to the office of auditor, and was succeeded by Mr. Thomas Hayward.

III.

And so, with eager hearts, directors looked forward to a rosy future. It is interesting to recall what, in their opinion, the financial prospects of the line were. Larger schemes loomed in ambitious minds, but, even confined to the local line along the Severn valley, the estimated revenue was as follows:—

Passengers £2,350

Coal £750

Lead, Copper, and Barytes Ore £1,700

Timber (chiefly used in working the mines) £900

Iron, Powder, and other articles used by miners £75

Lime for Agricultural and other purposes £900

Corn, Flour, and other Agricultural Produce £600

Cattle, Sheep, and other animals £300

Wool and Woollen Manufactures £225

General Merchandise and Shop Goods £250

Building Stone, Tiles, Bricks, etc. £200

Total £8,250

Estimating working expenses at 50 per cent., that left a surplus of £4,125, being nearly 7 per cent. per annum on £60,000, the required capital. With such a scheme the majority of the local owners readily expressed their agreement, and arrangements were made for cutting of the first sod, in a field which was to form the site of the Llanidloes station, on October 3rd, 1855. Mrs. Owen, of Glansevern, was invited to perform the ceremony, but, owing to what she regarded as a premature announcement of the fact in the "Shrewsbury Chronicle," that lady sent an advertisement to the journal announcing the postponement of the function. Pages of the Company's minute book were devoted to expressions of the Board's "utmost astonishment" and demands for explanations. Mrs. Owen was at no loss for material to furnish equally voluminous reply, the pith of which was that she was simply inspired by a desire to obtain time, both to secure the attendance of her influential friends and to inform herself of the financial position of the undertaking.

It was all a storm in a tea-cup, but it was a very severe storm while it lasted; and Mr. Whalley had to cut the sod himself, in a deluge of rain, taking occasion, however, in doing so, to express, in graceful terms, the disappointment felt at the absence of one "who had done so much to introduce improved means of communication through the county," a reference equally gracefully acknowledged by letter from Glansevern a few days later. "Up to the present period," wrote Mrs. Owen, "we have been strangers in this part of the county to the preparations necessary for inaugurating a railway, and it should not, therefore, be wondered at if our first attempt should not have been attended with perfect success; misapprehension, excess of zeal and inexperience might all lead to mistakes and errors, and it is not, perhaps, possible for us all to escape censure."

Perhaps not. At any rate, it was a philosophic conclusion, and it enabled the Board, with unruffled feathers, to proceed to the business of receiving tenders for the construction of the line. Out of seven, the lowest was that of Mr. David Davies, who was, moreover, prepared to accept part payment in shares, an arrangement which, later, paved the way to the process of leasing these local railways to the contractors, that became almost a custom. Hardly, however, had these preliminaries been successfully negotiated, when Mr. Rice Hopkins died, and after a temporary agreement with one of his relatives to carry on in an advisory capacity, the Board proceeded to select a successor out of four "persons who presented themselves as eligible for this purpose."

Their choice was easily made. The line was being built by a local contractor. Fate was now to throw up a new engineer, whose claims were not less obvious on similar grounds. A native of Trefeglwys, Mr. Benjamin Piercy had, from an early age, taken great interest in railway planning, and, though this branch of the profession did not directly touch his daily routine, he devoted many leisure hours to its study. In his journeys through Wales he was impressed with the necessity of opening out its valleys to the great railway world that was developing beyond the English border, and when Mr. Henry Robertson began to make his surveys of the Shrewsbury and Chester line, Mr. Piercy became one of his assistants. So diligently did the young man discharge his duties here that, it is recorded, he was the means of preventing the loss of a year in obtaining the Act for the making of this line.

It was natural, therefore, that, when the Rea Valley line was being mooted, he should be engaged to prepare the Parliamentary plans. It was in this connection that an untoward incident occurred, which throws some light on the tremendous rivalry that existed among the promoters of various railway schemes and the means that were sometimes adopted to thwart the progress of antagonistic proposals. Mr. Piercy had, with great energy, got his plans ready and taken them to London, but they were surreptitiously removed from his room at the hotel, and the matter was hung up for a year. In the meantime, as we have already noted, the line of route was changed. In the following year, however, he duly deposited the plans for the railway from Shrewsbury to Welshpool, with a branch to Minsterley, already mentioned. Although strongly opposed, at every stage, including Standing Orders, Mr. Piercy succeeded in carrying the Bill through both Houses, and it received the Royal assent. It was in the Select Committees on this Bill that he first made his reputation as a witness in Parliamentary Committees. After this he was engaged upon nearly all the projects for introducing independent railways into Wales, all of them meeting with fierce opposition. For several days consecutively he was as a witness under cross-examination by the genial Mr. Serjeant Merewether, and other eminent counsel, but so little headway were they able to make against Mr. Piercy that, upon one occasion, when a Committee passed a Bill of his, Mr. Merewether held up his brief-bag and asked the Committee whether they would not give that too to Mr. Piercy. [16]

The late MR. GEORGE OWEN,
Engineer of the Cambrian Railways for many years.

In 1858 Mr. Piercy was formally appointed engineer to the Company. With the assistance of Mr. George Owen, the cordial co-operation of Messrs. Davies and Savin, and under the enthusiastic leadership of Mr. Whalley, he was destined to carry these undertakings into being, and to nurture them in their infancy, and thus to join the little group of pioneer workers who, in their several capacities, may, in special degree, be termed the parents of the Cambrian.

CHAPTER II. A BIRTHDAY PARTY.

> "A birthday:—and now a day that rose
> with much of hope, with meaning rife—
> A thoughtful day from dawn to close."
>
> —JEAN INGLEOW.

With the advent of the young Montgomeryshire engineer, and his cordial co-operation with the Montgomeryshire contractor, the public began eagerly to count the days, or at any rate, the months, before the due arrival of the first Montgomeryshire railway. The prospects of a punctual delivery were eminently propitious. In his first report, Mr. Piercy was able to announce substantial progress with the work, which was being carried out by Messrs. Davies and Savin, "at a cost below that of any railway yet brought into operation." True, there were one or two inevitable set-backs. One of the engines which had arrived by road, and been set on the rails at Newtown, refused properly to perform its duty; but, fortunately, a Mr. Howell, of Hawarden, who knew all about the intricate interior of these new-fangled monsters, happened to be staying at Llanidloes, and he was called in to diagnose and advise, with effective result.

A more serious problem was the revision of the terms of the lease of the line to Messrs. Davies and Savin, which a committee of shareholders were busily engaged in attempting to carry forward. Complications of another sort led Mr. Piercy to tender his resignation, which, being somewhat peremptorily refused, he withdrew. Still further anxiety and considerable expense was involved in the prosecution of Parliamentary application for power to extend the line from the originally designed terminus at Newtown to the Shropshire Union Canal; for, though it was only a matter of some quarter of a mile, it was strenuously opposed in both Houses. Such were the distractions which beset railway building in those days; but enthusiasm and determination still triumphed, and the work proceeded along the line with sufficient rapidity to admit its being opened for mineral traffic on April 30th, 1859. At the very last moment trouble was experienced in obtaining the necessary certificate of the Board of Trade for passenger traffic, but that precious document came to hand on August 9th, and, with more fortunate outcome than on a previous occasion, Mrs. Owen, of Glansevern, was invited to perform the pleasing duty of declaring the line open.

The day fixed was Wednesday, August 31st, and a local newspaper gives us some account of the proceedings:—"Preparations were made on an extensive scale, and the day was ushered in by cannon firing, bell-ringing, and the hearty congratulations of the people of the town, with their country friends, who flocked in to take part in the proceedings. The houses were elegantly decorated with flags and banners, flowers and evergreens, and a variety of mottoes, more or less appropriate. Amongst others we noticed, on the Old Market Hall (which, by the way, it was a charity to hide from the gaze of strangers), a profusion of flags, with a large banner in the centre, 'Hail, Star of Brunswick.' The Red Lion exhibited a local tribute to its friend, by placing on the door 'Welcome, Whalley, champion of our rights.' The Railway Station was profusely decorated, and the Queen's Head displayed an elegant archway of leaves and flowers. The Trewythen Arms was also gaily covered with flags, and numbers of private houses displayed a variety of gay decorations. The cold and wet state of the weather in no way damped the ardour of the men of Montgomeryshire, and they were rewarded by a speedy dispersion of clouds, and the grateful warmth of the noonday sun. Llanidloes was all alive; business was entirely suspended and soon after 9 o'clock a large crowd collected near the public rooms, where a procession was formed, headed by the Plasmadoc Brass Band, and accompanied in the following order by:—

The Mayor (W. Swancott, Esq.), and the Corporation consisting of Messrs. R. Homes, E. Clayton, T. Davies, T. F. Roberts, D. Snead; L. Minshall, Pugh, J. Jarman, Hamer, J. Mendus Jones,

Flag.

Banner,—'Whither Bound?' 'To Milford.'

Streamer. Banner. Streamer.

(With the inscription):

'G. H. Whalley, whose unceasing exertions are now crowned with success.'

Mr. G. H. Whalley, Chairman.

Deputy Chairman and Secretary, Directors.

Banner,—'The spirited contractors, Messrs. Davies & Savin.'

Streamer. Streamer.

Banner,—'Our Esteemed Patroness, Mrs. A. W. Owen.'

Mrs. Owen followed in a carriage.

Guests and Shareholders.

Ladies (two and two).

Gentlemen (two and two).

Streamer. Streamer.

Banner,—'Prosperity to the Towns of Llanidloes and Newtown.'

Excavators (with bannerets).

Flag,—'Live and let Live.'

The Public.

"The procession was marshalled by Mr. Marpole Lewis, and after parading the streets, was met by Mrs. Owen, of Glansevern, who was accompanied by some lady friends and Mr. Brace, and at another point by Mr. Whalley, the chairman of the company. These arrivals were acknowledged with vociferous cheering. The procession, like a rolling snowball, gained bulk as it proceeded, and before it reached the station, comprehended a very large proportion of the inhabitants,—ladies and gentlemen,—with a good sprinkling of their neighbours. At the station there was a considerable delay, awaiting the arrival of the train from Newtown. At last it made its appearance, and the band struck up 'See the Conquering Hero comes,'—an air far more appropriate when applied to the 'locomotive' than to one-half of the heroes to whom it has hitherto done honour. The Mayor of Llanidloes, with the Corporation, Mrs. Owen and party, and Mr. Whalley, accompanied by a very large number of the inhabitants, then took their seats, and amidst the cheers of those left behind, and counter cheers of the passengers, the train moved off and proceeded slowly towards Newtown. [20]

"The train arrived shortly after 12 o'clock, when the procession re-formed and escorted the Mayor and Corporation of Llanidloes, Mrs. Owen, of Glansevern, Mr. Whalley, and other visitors, to Newtown Hall, where an elegant déjeuner had been provided by Dr. Slyman. The decorations at Newtown Hall were chaste and beautiful. The verandah at the front, was tastefully ornamented with flowers and evergreens, surmounted by a number of elegant fuschias, in the centre of which stood out a prettily worked 'Prince of Wales' Feathers.' A variety of flags were placed around the pleasure ground, which gave a very striking effect to the scene."

After the party had partaken of refreshments, there were toasts and mutual congratulations, and the procession tramped back to the station.

"Again there was a little delay, awaiting the train from Llanidloes (says our chronicler), and it was half-past three o'clock before The Train of the day fairly started. Filling the carriages and trucks was no joke. Admirable arrangements had been made, and the ladies were first accommodated with seats. One or two gentlemen did attempt to take their place before this arrangement was fully carried out, but they were very unceremoniously brought out again, amidst the ironical cheers of the outsiders. At last the forty-eight trucks and carriages were loaded, and, at a moderate estimate, we should say, 3,000 people were in the train. The two new engines, The Llewelyn and The Milford, were attached to the carriages, and were driven by Mr. T. D. Roberts and Mr. T. E. Minshall. Although the train was so heavily laden with passengers, there was a large crowd of people left to cheer as it slowly passed out of the Station. The appearance of this monster train was magnificent. More than 2,000 of the passengers were in open trucks, and at certain points, where there was a curve in the line, and a good sight could be obtained, the train, as it wound its way through the valley, presented a scene not easily to be erased from the memory.

"Soon after four o'clock Llanidloes Station was reached, and the passengers alighted amidst the shouts of the inhabitants, who had come to welcome them. A large circle was formed in the field adjoining the Station, and Mr. Whalley introduced to those assembled Mrs. Owen, of Glansevern, who declared the line to be opened."

It hardly required her stirring words to enlist the enthusiasm of the company concerning the economic change which the railways were to bring to Wales. Derelict acres were to be brought into cultivation; "the very central town of the ancient Principality," in which that ceremony was taking place, was to become the capital of a new prosperity, and as for Mr. Whalley, were not that day's proceedings "a chapter more honourable than any wreath of laurel that could be won on the battle field by success in war?" The plaudits of the assembled confirmed the sentiment, and "a rush was then made for the tent where the luncheon was provided. Here again the ladies had the same proper attention paid to them; the sterner sex was kept out until they could be accommodated with seats. After a short delay the tent was well filled with visitors, and upwards of 300 sat down to lunch. Grace was said by the Rector of Llanidloes, and for a season the clatter of knives and forks was the only sound to be heard."

Small wonder! For the afternoon was well advanced, and the time-table had gone rather awry. But that did not in the least damp the ardour of the company. Refreshed by their belated meal, more toasts were honoured, more speeches made, and the future continued to assume the most roseate hue. The district, declared one orator, was destined to become "the abode of smiling happiness," and Newtown and Llanidloes "the haunts and hives of social industry." It was, said another, the first link in a chain "which must, ere long, form one of the greatest and most important trunk lines in the kingdom." "People," exclaimed a third, "laughed at it because it had no head or tail"; but let the scoffers wait and see! With all these glowing anticipations, proceedings became so protracted that the ladies had to withdraw, but the gentlemen went on drinking toasts with undiminished energy. They drank to the Chairman; they drank to the Secretary; they drank to the Engineer, and the Contractors, and the Bankers who had lent them the money, and to the success of the other railways springing up around them, including the Mid-Wales, the first sod of which was to be cut in a few days' time, with what strange accompaniment will be noted in a subsequent chapter. Not until the health of the Press,—"may its perfect independence ever expose abuses and advocate what is just, through evil and through good report,"—had been duly honoured did the company disperse.

The workmen, too, were entertained, with good fare and more speeches. Salvers and cake baskets were presented to Messrs. Davies and Savin. Master Edward Davies, aged 5, and Master Tom Savin, aged 6, were held up aloft, and presented with watches, and the cheering, which had gone on almost continuously for hours, broke forth afresh. One of the workmen, who was also, at any rate, in the opinion of his colleagues, something of a poet, stepped forward, and, "amidst roars of laughter and tremendous cheering," sang his thanks as follows:—

>Well now we've got a railway,
> The truth to you I'll tell,
>To be opened in August,
> The people like it well;
>We've heard a deal of rumour
> O'er all the country wide,
>We'll never get a railway,
> The people can't provide.
>
>Well now we have the carriages,
> For pleasure trips to ride;
>The Milford it shall run us,
> And Henry lad shall drive;
>There's also Jack the stoker,
> So handy and so free,
>He lives now at Llandiman,
> A buxom lad is he.
>
>We have a first rate gentleman
> Who does very nigh us dwell,
>And he has got a partner,
> The people like him well;
>Look at the trucks my boys,
> Their names you'll plainly see;
>They've took another Railway,
> There's plenty of work for we.

Well now our gen'rous masters
  Do handsomely provide
A store of meat and drink my boys,
  Come out and take a ride;
For we are in our ribbons,
  And dress'd so neat and trim;
Drink up my charming Sally,
  We'll fill it to the brim.

When these few days are over,
  The navvies they will part,
And go back to their gangers
  With blithe and cheerful heart;
And Jack he will be hooting,
  And getting drunk full soon;
I wish there was a railway
To be opened every moon.

And now I have to finish,
  And shall conclude my song;
I hope and trust my good friends,
  I've stated nothing wrong;
All you young men and maidens,
  That are so full of play,
I hope you'll all take tickets
  On that most glorious day.

"When the song was concluded, Colonel Wynn purchased the first copy, for which the fortunate bard received a shilling. Several other gentlemen followed this example, and the poet must have regretted that his stock in trade was so limited.

"During the latter part of the proceedings, several had left the enclosure to join the merry dance, to the strains of the Welshpool Band, in the adjoining field. We cannot use the usual stock phrase of the penny-a-liner and say to 'trip it on the light fantastic toe,' for in several instances a pair of stalwart navvies might be seen in anything but dancing pumps kicking out most gloriously. In another part of the field, a party were deeply engaged in an exciting game of football. All was mirth and jollity. From the oldest to the youngest, the richest to the poorest, every one seemed to try to get as much enjoyment out of the evening as possible, and if there were any grumblers to be found at Messrs. Davies and Savin's monster picnic, the fault must have been with themselves.

"The same evening rejoicings were being kept up at Llanidloes. All the school children of the place were feasted in the tent. Mr. Whalley (the 'champion of the people's rights,' as the flag had it) was chaired through the town, and the evening was finished by a ball. And on the following day, several loaves of bread and gallons of porter were sent by Messrs. Davies and Savin to the poor people of Llandinam." Finally, a medal was struck in commemoration of the event, and presented to the workmen.

Thus, sixty-three years ago, did the community, already conscious of the momentous influence the steam engine was exerting upon the social and economic condition of the countryside, but yet to discover the not less remarkable potentialities of the electric or the petrol spark applied to the problems of transport, herald the birth of the infant Cambrian.

CHAPTER III. EARLY DEVELOPMENTS AND DIFFICULTIES.

> "We may perceive plenty of wrong turns taken at cross roads, time misused or wasted, gold taken for dross and dross for gold, manful effort mis-directed, facts misread, men misjudged. And yet those who have felt life no stage play, but a hard campaign with some lost battles, may still resist all spirit of general insurgence in the evening of their day."—VISCOUNT MORLEY OF BLACKBURN.

Though one or two earlier bubbles, blown by eager railway promoters, had burst almost as they left the bowl of the pipe, the issue of the prospectus of the Montgomeryshire Railways Company, in 1852, not unnaturally inspired new hope in the border counties of some extension of already projected lines in the locality. At Oswestry, in particular, there was a rapidly growing feeling that such a development was overdue, and they looked with eager eyes towards the possibility of forging a connecting link with the system growing up in the heart of Powysland. The Shrewsbury and Chester Railway, soon to become part of the Great Western, had opened its branch to the busy Shropshire market centre under the hills at the beginning of 1849,—the year which saw the birth of the Oswestry Market and of the "Oswestry Advertizer," which, in its earlier years, was to devote so many pages to the record of the making of the Cambrian. But beyond Oswestry travellers had to proceed by coach. The "Royal Oak," leaving the town daily at one o'clock, arrived at Newtown about five. Goods were carried by more ponderous road transport, and it is rather astonishing to recal that as late as 1853 dogs were employed as draught animals, and local records include the circumstance of the death of a "respected tradesman" by a fall from his horse, caused by the animal's "fright at one of the carts drawn by the dogs, which are much too often seen on the roads in this neighbourhood." Legislation was soon to prohibit this custom, and railways to make it unnecessary.

Some early Chairmen

It was, then, in an Oswestry of very different social habits to those of to-day that, on June 23rd, 1853, the townspeople assembled at the call of the Mayor, Mr. William Hodges, to consider the question of a possible extension of the "Montgomeryshire Railway," in their direction, which was declared by resolution to be the "only scheme before Parliament capable of effecting this most desirable object."

But railways are not built by resolution alone, or the whole countryside would soon have become heavy with steam. As a matter of fact, it soon was, but not the sort of steam which drives locomotives or urges on the progress of practical railway construction. Ever since 1844, reliance had been placed in the possibility of assistance from one or both of the great lines which already had access to the Welsh border. Hope was first centred in the North Western, which had designs on a line from Shrewsbury into Montgomeryshire, but, in the Oswestry area, wistful eyes turned towards Paddington, and in propitiation of expected favours to come, four men with Great Western interests,—Mr. W. Ormsby-Gore, who became its first chairman; Sir Watkin, who later succeeded him in the chair; Col. Wynn, M.P., and Mr. Rowland James Venables,—were placed on the Oswestry and Newtown Board. The Earl of Powis, though a "North Westerner," was found to be not without ready desire to look at things all round. He was for a line to Shrewsbury, and also a line to Oswestry, but not to Oswestry alone. Even the line to Oswestry, according to North Western notions, was to be a branch either from Garthmyl or Criggion, according to whether the Shrewsbury and Montgomeryshire line went by the Rea Valley or by Alberbury, and that was not at all to Oswestrian taste. In the end, however, his lordship agreed to support the Oswestry project, and to take the value of his land,—some £10,000,—in shares, provided the possessor of Powis Castle was allowed to nominate a director, as the owner of Wynnstay was on the Great Western Board. The condition was readily granted, and the Oswestry and Newtown Bill, freed from North Western opposition, was allowed to pass. It obtained Royal Assent on June 26th, 1855, and the first general meeting was held at Welshpool on July 21st of that year.

Local rivalries, however, were not so easily dispelled. Welshpool's impartiality as between the Shrewsbury and the Oswestry lines was anathema at the latter town, where Mr. Whalley, speaking for nearly an hour and a half, readily persuaded a great meeting to register its insistence on the Oswestry scheme as an extension of the Llanidloes and Newtown, and so form another link in the chain that was to bind Manchester and Milford. Anyhow, Oswestry must be made "the initial town and not Newtown." In support of this the local promoters looked for substantial aid from the Great Western. But that company proved singularly unready to render any assistance. "Not only," said Mr. Abraham Howell, in giving evidence before Lord Stanley's Committee some years later, "did the Great Western not aid in the capital for the Oswestry, but they did not support the Shrewsbury. On the contrary they opposed it with all their efforts at every step. They also, by a manœuvre which their position of power over the Oswestry Company and their railway experience enabled them to carry out, succeeded in separating the Shrewsbury from the main line, and causing it to drift into the hands of the North Western. They, on the day of, or immediately before the Wharncliffe meeting of the Oswestry Company, got their friends to pay into the bankers in respect of their shares, and give their proxies to the extent of the ¼th in money, against the clauses in the Shrewsbury bill, by which it was intended to connect it with the Oswestry. By this means they cut off from the Welsh line their head and outlet at Shrewsbury, leaving them with the Oswestry head only, to which place they, the Great Western, alone had access, and therefore, under their exclusive power; a result which proved highly detrimental to the Oswestry and the Welshpool lines. During the five years from 1855 to 1859 the advantage given to the Great Western interest placed our company practically under their control."

Small wonder that public impatience began to show signs of strain. Cynical allusions appeared in the Press. "The only danger in making oneself liable for new schemes," wrote one captious critic, "arises from the possibility of their being proceeded with." Not even the "glorious news" of the fall of Sebastopol sufficed to deflect the local mind from the irritating habits of a dilatory directorate. After all, the Crimea was a long way off,—much further than Chirk,—to which place, the Great Western Company, on taking over the Shrewsbury and Chester line, had, under the profession of "revising" the fares, substantially raised them. This habit is one to which the community has become more accustomed in recent years, but that was a first experience of the ways of powerful monopolists, and it effectively emphasised the contention that it was high time "an independent" railway company, more directly under local control, should materialise.

Addresses were exchanged between Oswestry and Welshpool, much after the manner of diplomatic "Notes," some of them phrased in the spirited language which diplomats know so well how to cloak in conventional formulas. Occasionally even the conventional formulas were dispensed with. Questions concerning the legality of certain assemblies were pugnaciously raised and as pugnaciously answered. Four hours' somewhat heated discussion at an extraordinary meeting of shareholders at Welshpool carried matters no further than the decision that the first sod, when it was cut, should be of Montgomeryshire soil, "but whether," adds a critical commentator, "at Llanymynech, Welshpool or Newtown, no one knows." Fresh controversy arose concerning the secretaryship, to which office Mr. Princep had been appointed by Mr. Ormsby-Gore, after a very fleeting appearance on the kaleidoscopic scene of a Mr. Farmer, and the old rivalry of Great Western and North Western "interests" re-appeared in fresh form. The "Oswestry Advertizer," pointing the warning finger at the fate of another Welsh railway which, after £25,000 out of a total capital of £400,000 had been raised, found everything "swallowed up in the gulph of Chancery" under the winding-up Acts, proclaimed,—"We are almost afraid the Oswestry and Newtown is doomed to the same end." It certainly looked as if a true prophet was writing that dirge!

"It is hardly possible," says Mr. Howell, "to conceive a more deplorable state than that to which the company was reduced during this period of five years of Great-western regime. Every shilling that could be realized of the proceeds of a very superior share list was expended, debt was accumulated, every resource was exhausted; but comparatively little was done in the execution of the works; the company was involved in four chancery suits, of large proportions, and a law suit, and with other suits in prospect. It was necessary to provide £45,000 in cash, towards relieving the chairman from a personal liability of £75,000, and to let free the action of the company from the chancery suits; also further sums to discharge the claims of the contractors and carry on the works." So moribund, indeed, did the whole affair seem, that the North Western, treating it as practically extinct, began to consider a scheme for converting the Shropshire Union Canal, already in their hands, as a railway to Newtown!

And here were the promoters of this ill-starred project fighting amongst themselves. One party was for keeping back the line from Oswestry till, as a newspaper writer put it, "a rival to Shrewsbury is brought into condition to do it damage." Another was for complicating it with other new schemes. One of the sternest of all controversies still raged round the moot point whether the line was to run from Oswestry to Newtown or from Newtown to Oswestry, and even private friends fell out as to the exact spot on the proposed route at which the actual work should begin! "Discord triumphs—local prejudice is rampart—personal ill-will abounds—as a necessary consequence no one will apply for the unappropriated shares. Dissolution alone is imminent," cries the distracted editor.

It was certainly becoming apparent that this was no time for further dallying. The Shrewsbury and Welshpool undertaking, it was reported, was enlisting "an amount of public interest and support seldom equalled in the history of railways," and early in 1856 the directors of the Oswestry and Newtown line found it expedient to assure the community that "preparations for letting the contract were in active progress" and the first sod was to be cut on April 11th. Alas for the optimism of eager pioneers and the credulity of an impatient public! April 11th came and proved nothing else than a slightly belated "All Fools Day"! No sod was cut. Not a spade or a barrow was visible, and the operation might, by all appearances be postponed till the Greek Kalends. Patience, already sorely tried, became utterly exhausted. In June the Shrewsbury and Welshpool Railway Bill was read a third time in the House of Commons, and thus the rival scheme loomed still larger upon the horizon. Men had yet to learn that railways could be co-operative as well as competitive.

But so fully, indeed, was the popular mind at that time obsessed with the rivalry of routes that a rumour was started imputing to the directors of the Oswestry and Newtown Company the intention of "disuniting the line between Oswestry and Welshpool." As if there were not disunion enough already! More genial humorists launched the story that the Prince of Wales was coming down expressly to cut the first sod and had ordered a new pair of "navvys" for the occasion to be made by a Welshpool bootmaker. Feeling, however, was rising again, which was not moderated by the apologia of the directorate suggestive that it was all due to differences between them and the engineers. The engineers themselves were more or less at variance, and, in April 1856, Mr. Barlow, the chief, finding it impossible to agree with his assistant, Mr. Piercy, resigned.

Matters had come to so critical a juncture that eventually, by some happy inspiration, a "committee of investigation" was appointed to examine "the affairs, position and financial state of the Company." The Rev. C. T. C.

Luxmoore was elected to preside at this inquiry with Mr. Peploe Cartwright of Oswestry as his deputy, and they issued a voluminous report containing a series of recommendations, of which one of the most interesting is that, to reduce expenditure, the earthworks should be limited to a single line, "in all other respects making preparations for a double line." That, as travellers over the Cambrian to-day are aware, save for the length between Oswestry and Llanymynech, and between Buttington and Welshpool on the Oswestry and Newtown section, was eventually the course adopted. Bridges, including those over the Vyrnwy at Llanymynech, and the Severn at Pool Quay, were built with an extra span for a second pair of rails, but the girders still remain without further completion. The directors did not escape pointed reference to their "heavy responsibilities," but there was at least the "consolitary fact" that, despite enormous expenditure already incurred, "provided the arrears of deposit, calls and interest are paid up, a sum of £60,000 over and above the Parliamentary deposit of £18,000 invested in the hands of the Accountant-General, will be at once available for the works, an amount little short of sufficient to form half the line," and the shareholders are urged, "manfully confronting the difficulties that present themselves" to "merge all local jealousies and differences of opinion, in a hearty and unanimous effort to carry out the works."

It is a long and tortuous story and well may a journalist of those days, bemoan the perplexity of the local historian "when he turns over the files of the various newspapers, to see in one number the praises of certain gentlemen sung by admiring editors and enthusiastic correspondents, and in the next frantic outbursts from distracted shareholders against the devoted heads of the same gentlemen, who, but one short week before were the admired of all the shareholding admirers. One week he would find a noble lord wafted to the skies on the breath of a public meeting, but in the next 'the breath thus vainly spent' would blow his lordship up in a very different fashion, and those whose cheers had wafted my lord to that elevated position, would fain keep him there, so that sublunary affairs as far as regarded railways, would be out of his reach. Then he would find another gentleman on the directory, one day the idol and leading speaker of every meeting, called on the next a 'strife-engendering-judge,' and his place filled by another on the board. Presto! and this same gentleman, again turns up trumps! A professional gentleman is the pet of the whole company, but speedily a woe is pronounced upon lawyers. Again the wheel turns round, and the solicitor's great exertions and painstaking attention to the interests of the line are acknowledged." [34]

"Our historian would next discover 'much talkee' (as John Chinaman would say) anent a certain, or rather uncertain, 'blighting influence' which arrested the progress of some of the works, and to get to the bottom of which a 'committee of investigation' was appointed. He would open his eyes when he saw the revelations made by that committee, and would wonder how in the name of fortune—or misfortune—the shareholders could be such 'geese' (to apply a term used by one of the best directors the line ever had) as to allow affairs to go on as they had done. He would find that committee triumphant in the praises of the people, but snubbed by another committee who conducted the ceremony of cutting a first sod that would not have been cut this century but for them. When the investigation committee's work was ended (but not finished!) he would find rival claimants for honour:—Mr. Soandso here, Mr. Whatshisname there, and other gentlemen elsewhere discovering that they were the 'saviours of the line'—'unravellers of the mystery' while the line was yet in jeopardy, and the mystery as dark as Erebus. He would then go on to disputes with contractors and engineers, a law suit commenced here, and threatened there,—directors retiring, and shareholders well-nigh at their wits end. Lawyers are again at a 'Premium' and three are appointed to lay their heads together in order to make heads of agreement, for the guidance of new contractors, while the old ones, who the shareholders were afraid would sack the company, were themselves sacked!"

That, indeed, is the usual fate of those who attempt to follow dead controversies through their never-ending labyrinths. A sentimental historian has said that "the world is full of the odour of faded violets"; but, in looking back over these yellow pages of the past, the scent which greets us is sometimes hardly as fragrant; and were it not for purposes of comprehensive record, many of these acrid, but not unamusing, incidents might be decently left buried in oblivion. Happily, however, even the battle of the Oswestry and Newtown Railway was not eternal. The day dawned on which it was gleefully acclaimed that the directors had at length "caught the spirit of promptitude from the committee" and before long "it might be expected to see hundreds of navvies engaged in cutting up the earth." Storm clouds might re-gather later, as we shall see, but for the time being peace was restored.

Differences as to policy and even as to the site of the sod cutting were sufficiently composed by the summer of 1857 to admit of a start being made with the work of construction, and on Tuesday, August 4th, the initial ceremony, performed by Lady Williams Wynn, took place, in a field on the east side and adjoining the bowling green at Welshpool. The spot bears no mark to-day, as it might well do, but it may be mentioned that it is between the rails on the down line, as you enter Welshpool station from Buttington, just opposite the signal box. There were, needless to say, great public rejoicings. The long delay in getting to the actual stage of operations gave additional zest to the popular acclaim when that point had, at last, been really reached, and the proceedings were of the most effective and striking character. Crowds flocked in from all sides. Montgomery shared fully in the popular acclamation, and only Oswestry, among the interested towns, stood somewhat aloof. The question of "priority," apparently, still rankled, and "some misunderstanding" spoilt the effect of what was intended to be a general business holiday. "Only two or three shops were closed, while the others remained open as usual," and some of the more prominent Oswestry shareholders were conspicuous by their absence at the ceremony, at which no reference was made to the expediting influence of the "committee of investigation."

SOD CUTTING CEREMONY OF THE OSWESTRY AND NEWTOWN RAILWAY AT WELSHPOOL ON AUGUST 10, 1857.

But in Welshpool the streets were bright with bunting. At noon shops were closed in order that everyone might participate in the ceremonial. Bells pealed from the Church tower; cannon, "captured at Seringapatam by the great Lord Clive" were fired from Powys Castle, and a committee, headed by the Mayor (Mr. Owen, grandfather of Mr. Robert Owen of Broad Street), who had taken an active interest in the promotion of both the Oswestry and Shrewsbury lines, assisted by the Town Clerk, carried the day's programme through in triumph, which included the inevitable "procession."

A contemporary record may here supply us with the necessary details:— "The Procession began to form in the Powis Castle Park. After some little delay it proceeded towards the Bowling Green, in the following order:—

Two Marshals, on Horseback.

A body of the Montgomeryshire Yeomanry Cavalry dismounted.

The Band.

The Mayor and High Sheriff.

Aldermen and Town Councillors of the Borough of Welshpool.

The wheel-barrow to be used by Lady Williams Wynn, in performing the ceremony.

The Directors of the Company.

The Officials.

Shareholders and Well-wishers.

Band of the Royal Montgomeryshire Rifles.

School Children,—including the National School, Infant Girl and Boys' School and others.

Flags.

The First Friendly Society.

Flags and Banners.

The Second Friendly Society.

Flags and Banners.

Third Friendly Society.

Flags and Banners.

Cambrian Friendly Society.

Flags and Banners.

A small body of the Royal Montgomeryshire Rifles.

"This possession extended to a very considerable length, and was followed by an immense concourse of pleasure-seekers and others who had come to the town for the purpose of witnessing the ceremony.

"The body of Yeomanry Cavalry were selected by Sergeant-Major Turner, as a body-guard for Lady Wynn during the ceremony, and being in full dress presented a very creditable appearance.

THE CEREMONY.

"At about one o'clock the procession arrived at the spot where the ceremony was to be performed. This, we have stated before, was on the east side of the Bowling Green, on the part of the mound on that side of the green facing the spot, seats were placed which were occupied by anxious and eager spectators.

"After the procession had been properly arranged around the spot, the ceremony was at once proceeded with," not the least impressive item in it being the solemn invocation by Archdeacon Clive that "God would bless the undertaking in the name of His Son Jesus Christ." The Mayor then presented Lady Wynn with a copy of the programme of the day's proceedings printed in gold letters on blue silk; Mrs. Owen of Glansevern read a learned address dipping deep in the classical history of transport, "the first sod was then cut by Lady Wynn, with the silver spade placed in the wheelbarrow provided by the contractor, and wheeled by her along the planks laid on the ground, in a very graceful manner. Her ladyship performed the ceremony amidst the deafening applause of the assembled multitude. Afterwards other ladies and gentlemen, including the directors, contractors, engineers, etc., went through the same ceremony, using a common wheelbarrow.

"The wheelbarrow, made of mahogany, was emblazoned with the seal of the company, while on the silver spade was engraved the following:—

> "Presented to Lady Watkin Williams Wynn, by the Contractor of the Oswestry and Newtown Railway, on the occasion of turning the first sod, at Welchpool, on Tuesday, the 4th of August, 1857."

"Under the inscription was a copy of the seal of the company."

Subsequently a "cold collation" was provided in a tent on the Bowling Green; there was a prolific toasting of everybody, or nearly everybody concerned, and what was felt to be one of the most auspicious days in the annals of Powysland closed with rural sports and dancing. That night the shareholders dreamt of prodigious dividends.

CHAPTER IV. OSWESTRY TO NEWTOWN.

> "But a child,
> Yet in a go-cart. Patience; give it time
> There is a hand that guides.
>
> —BENNETT COLL.

It is easy to-day to smile at the optimism of our grand-fathers. We know now that railway dividends are not as readily earned in real life as they sometimes are in dreams which follow gorgeous banquets; but, in one respect, at any rate, the future of the Oswestry and Newtown undertaking appeared to justify jubilation. Axes had been, at any rate, temporarily buried; the advocates of rival routes had composed their differences and everything pointed to a rapid consummation of the scheme. As a matter of fact, little delay was experienced in getting to work with the actual construction. Before October opened gangs of labourers were busy on the track between Pant and Llandysilio. The original idea of a broad gauge line, similar to that adopted by Brunel on the Great Western's southern arm, had been abandoned in favour of what has since become the standard one for this country of 4ft. 8½ins. [40]

Nevertheless, it was no small undertaking. The Vyrnwy had to be crossed at Llanymynech and the Severn at Pool Quay and again near Buttington. The rest of the line was comparatively free from serious engineering problems, but fresh Parliamentary powers had to be obtained to construct a branch from Llynclys to the Porthywaen lime quarries, and even a little addition of this sort involved endless correspondence over details and other wearing worries. Difficulties of another sort, more formidable, began to appear. The Earl of Powis, whose influence counted for so much, expressing regret for certain differences which had arisen in relation to the policy of the Board, wrote to Sir Watkin resigning his seat, adding the warning note, "I think you should for your own sake watch somewhat jealously the proceedings with regard to the contract." Sir Watkin hastened to assure his lordship of the "grief and astonishment" which his withdrawal had occasioned his colleagues and to deprecate divisions at critical hours.

And it certainly was a critical hour. Money was urgently wanted, borrowing was barred until provisions of the Act were complied with, and though an attempt by Mr. Barlow to seek an injunction in Chancery failed after a hard struggle, the contract had to be dissolved in order to substitute an arrangement by which payment could be made by shares and debentures in lieu of cash. It was on this account that Messrs. Davidson and Oughterson, who had earlier succeeded Messrs. Thornton and McCormick, in turn gave place to the men who had already come to the rescue of the Newtown and Llanidloes undertaking.

The arrangements by which these early undertakings were "leased" to the contractors has been the subject of controversy among railway financial experts, but they were stoutly defended in a letter to the "Times" shortly after the completion of most of them by Mr. David Davies himself, who claimed that by this means "Wales had the benefit of something like 700 miles of railway which would not have been made for at least another century if we had waited for the localities to subscribe the necessary funds." In the present case, at any rate, Mr. Savin's efforts at financial re-establishment were the outcome of the suggestion of the North Western, warmly supported by the Great Western party, including the Chairman himself, who had become practically liable for £75,000, if the railway was not made and the company set upon a sound footing. To set free the powers of the Company no less than £45,000 had to be paid down, no small task with subscriptions to the share list not easy to obtain. Yet, that Mr. Savin accomplished—and more. He bought up the existing contract, compromised and settled all existing claims and got rid of all liabilities. The rearrangement, however, took a great deal of time, and was later complicated by the dissolution of partnership between him and Mr. Davies, while the works were proceeding between Welshpool and Newtown. Not until July 26th, 1861, was it finally arranged that Mr. Savin should relinquish the lease, and work the line on an amended basis, under which he was to take the earnings, pay 4¾ per cent. to the Company, supplementing the earnings of the line by a draft upon the North Western, who granted rebates. [42]

Still, it considerably expedited construction. The works came into the new hands in October 1859, and so far as the chief portions of the undertaking went, progress became quite satisfactory. As is so often the case, in these affairs, it was an unexpected development over a detail that caused the greatest perturbation. Another difference arising on the board, this time regarding certain engagements entered into about the site of the station at Oswestry, Sir Watkin, who appears to have had certain misgivings as to the conduct of the business, being out-voted at a meeting of the directors, just before Mr. Savin came into possession of the works, in his turn left the room and a few days later sent in his resignation. He was replaced in the chair by Mr. David Pugh, M.P., of Llanerchyddol Hall, Welshpool, who continued to act in that capacity till, on his death in 1861, he was succeeded by Mr. Whalley.

On the line, however, the navvies went doggedly digging on, despite atrocious weather. By May 1st, 1860, the track was sufficiently complete from Oswestry to Pool Quay to be opened for traffic to that point, and advertisements began to appear announcing "cheap trains" for excursionists to the "far-famed and commanding heights of Llanymynech Hills." In the middle of the month a more venturesome journey was attempted and, by the grace of God, safely accomplished. The last link in the iron road had just been laid, a mile or two from Welshpool, and one fine evening, "shortly after six o'clock" (as a local journalist records) "the 'Montgomery' was attached to a number of trucks, with rough seats placed on them for the occasion. Every available space was filled by a number of Poolonians who were in waiting. The train then slowly proceeded along the beautiful valley of the Severn to the Cefn Junction [43] (that is to be) with the Shrewsbury and Welshpool line, where more trucks were attached, and a considerable addition to the passengers made. Soon Welshpool was reached, and the shrill whistle of the engine—for the first time heard in that beautiful locality—was all but overpowered by the cheers of the assembled people. The train was brought to a standstill on the very spot where, some years ago (we are afraid to say how many) the first sod was cut. Congratulations were passed, and crowds of the very old, and the very young, to whom an Engine heretofore had been a figment of imagination, gazed with wonder at 'The Montgomery' while their more travelled neighbours adjourned to the Bowling Green, where Mr. R. Owen made a short pithy speech. He very properly acknowledged the business-like activity of Messrs. Davies and Savin, to whom the public were so largely indebted for the arrival of a locomotive at Welshpool. Mr. Webb, on behalf of the contractors, suitably responded; and the proceedings were cut short by a warning whistle from the engine, on which sat Campbell, the locomotive superintendent, who very prudently wished to get back over the rough road before the shades of evening overtook them. The train then went off for Pool Quay at a smart pace, considering that the rails were unballasted, and with the trucks loaded with juveniles, many of whom perhaps had this day their first trip by railway. In Welshpool the bells rang out merry peals, and cannons were fired, and everything betokened the hilarity of the inhabitants."

What the Board of Trade would say nowadays to a heavily-ladened train of passengers being run at a "smart pace," or any other, over an "unballasted" road, can be left to the reader's imagination!

Anyhow, the line being finally finished off to the last nut and bolt, was soon approved of by the Government Inspector, Colonel Yolland; and everything was ready for the formal opening on Tuesday, August 14th. "The day (says a contemporary account) proved most auspicious. Early in the morning the weather was very dull, but before the middle of the day it cleared up, and turned out most bright and cheerful. At about a quarter to eleven o'clock the Mayor and Corporation of Welshpool met at the Town Hall, and from thence proceeded (headed by the Montgomeryshire Yeomanry Band) to the Railway Station by eleven, in time for the train that was to convey them, together with the directors, shareholders, and general public to Oswestry.

"As may be readily supposed, a monster train was required for this purpose, and an immense number of carriages were in readiness. After some delay, the passengers took their seats, and the train started for Oswestry. The Corporation were followed by the Montgomeryshire Militia Band, and the 2nd Montgomeryshire Rifle Volunteers, who proceeded to Oswestry by the same train.

"As the train proceeded on its course, and arrived at the various stations, it was hailed with the most enthusiastic greetings from those who assembled along the line as spectators on this occasion.

"The arrival of the train at Oswestry was made the signal for a general discharge of artillery, such as is customarily used on these occasions, and added to this was the discharge of a great number of fog-signals. The bells of the Old Church, too, rang out their merriest peals. At the Station an immense concourse of people had assembled, and the Welshpool Corporation was received by the Mayor and Corporation of Oswestry, who had been escorted to the Station by the Rifle Corps, headed by their band. The Pool Corporation received a hearty greeting from their civic brethren in Oswestry, and the Montgomeryshire Rifles formed in column opposite the Oswestry Corps, and each presented arms, when the Oswestry Band struck up "God save the Queen." They all then proceeded, in the following order, to the Powis Hall:—

Banner. Banner.

Band and Members of the Oswestry Rifle Corps.

Band and Members of the 2nd Montgomeryshire Rifle Corps.

Band of the Montgomeryshire Yeomanry.

The Mayor and Corporation of Welshpool.

The Mayor and Corporation of Oswestry.

Tradesmen, Shareholders, etc.

Drum and Fife Band.

Navvies, etc.

"At the Town Hall the Corporation had most hospitably provided for their refreshment. Punch and wine of the choicest and best descriptions were abundantly supplied, under the management of Mr. Atkins, and Mrs. Edwards, of the Queen's Head Hotel, Oswestry. The company present included the Oswestry Corporation, the Welshpool Corporation, the directors of the railway, the Second Montgomeryshire Volunteers, and the Oswestry Volunteers."

The special train then returned to Welshpool, where Mrs. Owen of Glansevern declared the line opened. Then the inevitable procession, and the not less inevitable "cold collation" and speech making, and dancing. Only one untoward incident marked the day. Owing to the crush to board the returning train from Oswestry, the Montgomeryshire Yeomanry and Montgomeryshire Militia bands got left behind, and the Oswestry Rifle Corps musicians, who had been more successful in the scramble, had to do all the blowing for their stranded comrades. But, it is recorded, they blew with triple vigour, as well they might!

Oswestry was now, at long last, connected with Montgomeryshire, but there were those who felt in no mood for rejoicing in that event. Among the residents of the Severn Valley were those who, like the redoubtable Mr. Weller "considered that the rail is unconstitootional and an invader o' privileges." They solemnly shook their heads and deplored the doom of the mail-coach. What, they asked, was to become of Tustin? Tustin had driven the mail coach from Shrewsbury every morning, summer and winter, starting from the Post Office at 4 a.m., and covering the score of miles to Welshpool in about two hours. To see him and his fine horses arrive at the Royal Oak was a source of daily pride to Welshpolonians. "In the summer mornings," says a writer in the "Licensing Victualler's Gazette" in 1878, looking back upon those days, "there was always a number of people up to see the mail arrive, and the cordial and cheery welcome given to those passengers who alighted to partake of breakfast at the hotel, by the buxom and genial landlady, Mrs. Whitehall, was a thing to be remembered and talked about. She was the pink of what such a woman should be, and the fame of her cuisine reached very far beyond the county in which she lived." Later in the morning, the thirteen miles between Welshpool and Newtown were done in little more than an hour. But "the days of coaching were drawing to a close even in Wales; the iron horse was slowly to elbow one coach and then another off the road, putting them back as it were, nearer and nearer to the coast; until even Tustin and his famous Aberystwyth mail had to succumb. But they made a gallant fight of it, and died what we may call gamely." In recent years the coach, or its modern counterpart, the charabanc and motor bus, have come into something of their own again, and are providing, in turn, a new form of competition with the railways.

In 1860, long distance highway traffic did seem doomed, for the "iron horse" could cover the ground in what then appeared a prodigious pace. Six trains ran each way between Oswestry and Welshpool on week-days and two each way on Sundays, while excursion fares advertised in connection with a Sunday School trip from Oswestry to Welshpool held out the alluring advantage of "covered carriages, 1s.; first-class, 2s." for the double journey—a figure to make the mouth of the present day passenger water! It was hardly so necessary then, as it has proved to be on recent occasions, to the writer's personal knowledge, for groups of mourners travelling to a funeral to contrive to save a few pence by taking "pleasure party" tickets!

But, as yet, no "pleasure" or any other party could proceed by rail beyond Welshpool. Work on the remaining link, had begun; but at the Newtown end, where arrangements had been entered into for a working alliance with the Newtown and Llanidloes Railway. At the Welshpool end circumstances were not so propitious. The original surveys had been made by way of Berriew, but this necessitated carrying the line through part of the Glansevern domain, and, as the late Earl of Powis had jocularly remarked, in connection with the planning of a neighbouring line, the beau ideal of a railway is one that comes about a mile from one's own house and passes through a neighbour's land.

KILKEWYDD BRIDGE, near Welshpool,
as recently re-built.
Reproduced from the "Great Western Magazine."

So it was to the other side of the valley that Mr. Piercy had, at length, to carry his measuring instruments, and, crossing the Severn at Kilkewydd, climb the long incline to Forden. Before this was finally accomplished the dissolution of partnership between the contractors had taken place, and while Mr. Davies transferred his attention to some adjacent railway schemes, Mr. Savin took into partnership Mr. Ward of the Donnett, Whittington, near Oswestry, and the name of "Savin and Ward" was, for some years, to become as familiar in the railway world as had previously been that of "Davies and Savin." The four mile stretch between Newtown and Abermule was in working order and trains were running over this isolated section of the Oswestry and Newtown system, but the remaining gap between Abermule and Welshpool had still to receive its finishing touches, when the term set in the agreement for completion expired.

Mr. Savin was able to cite not only the "worst weather that anyone can remember," but the procrastination over the arrangement and transfer of the lease as ample justification for the delay in fulfilling the engagement. Moreover, other matters were arising which tended to distract the attention of the directors from any passing squabble as to dates. The "overbearing leviathians" might have been quelled some years earlier, but they had not been killed, and at the beginning of 1861, movements were again afoot in North-Western circles to secure an extension of the Minsterley branch to Montgomery, while under the Bishop's Castle Railway Bill, which was going through the Committee of the House of Lords, the London and North Western Railway, apparently trading on the payment made to the Oswestry and Newtown Company for access to Welshpool by way of Buttington, sought a further reciprocal arrangement by which, if the Oswestry and Newtown availed themselves of the powers to subscribe to, lease, or work the Bishop's Castle line, the North Western was to obtain the right to run over the Oswestry and Newtown metals into Newtown, the latter Company being given a quid pro quo in the shape of similar advantage over the Shrewsbury and Welshpool line. It seemed an innocent enough proposal on the surface, but it did not blind the astute Mr. Whalley to the danger of certain developments favourable to North Western interests. The clause, as it happened, had been inserted in the absence of any representatives of the Oswestry and Newtown Company, and this objection was carried into the committee room. For hours the arguments swayed to and fro. Numbers of witnesses, including officials of the Oswestry and Newtown, gave evidence; and, in the end, the anticipated compromise was affected, by withdrawals all round. The Bishop's Castle Railway lost the support of the Oswestry and Newtown, but the sinister designs of the North Western upon Newtown were finally scotched, and the local Company, of which Mr. Robert B. Elwin was now General Manager, and Mr. B. Tanner, who had not long succeeded Mr. Hayward, on his resignation, in that capacity on the Llanidloes and Newtown, secretary, could go forward with greater confidence.

On Monday, May 27th, the first train, drawn by the engine "Leighton," and conveying a party of invited guests and the engineers, passed safely over Kilkewydd bridge, amidst a fusillade of fog signals, and thus the last and most formidable of the engineering exploits on the new length of line was accomplished. The bridge had been constructed in remarkably short time, and a contemporary record of this auspicious incident duly mentions that "the speedy completion of so complicated and troublesome a task is mainly due to the indefatigable exertions of Mr. John Ward, one of the contractors, and Mr. James Marshall, the resident superintendent." Early the next month Colonel Yolland inspected the whole length from Welshpool to Newtown, pausing to express his special approbation of the Kilkewydd bridge [51] as "the best constructed on the line," and it was now open to the Company publicly to announce that from June 10th a through service of trains would run from Oswestry to Newtown and on to Llanidloes.

No further formal opening seems to have been arranged, but, though the day was, like so many that had so proceeded it, very wet, rapidly organised celebrations took place at some spots. Montgomery had already taken its share in the opening to Welshpool, but it was now to have a festival of its own, as was only fitting, since that ancient borough may, in no small sense, be regarded as one of the ancestral homes of the "Cambrian." It was here, as we have seen, that Mr. Piercy had largely acquired his interest and skill in railway engineering, while at the office of Mr. Charles Mickleburgh. A committee, with Mr. W. Mickleburgh as hon. secretary, and treasurer, had little difficulty in getting together some £150 as a celebration fund. A programme was as quickly organised, including, of course, a procession and a dinner, but to this was added another little ceremony,—the presentation by Mrs. Owen of Glansevern, now a familiar central figure on these occasions, of a silver bugle to Captain Johns and his gallant men of the Railway Volunteers. The instrument bore the inscription,—"Presented by Anne Warburton Owen, of Glansevern, to the Third Montgomeryshire (Railway) Rifles, 1861." Above was an appropriate design, on the dexter side a representation of the locomotive engine "Glansevern," and on the sinister a railway viaduct with a train passing over.

The occasion was singularly appropriate, for no small part in the initiation and maintenance of the Corps belongs to the little group of railway men who were associated with Montgomery, the Mickleburghs, Mr. George Owen, Mr. Piercy and others. In after years it was the habit of their children to ask these gallant men whether they had "ever really killed anyone" with their formidable swords, and some of them were wont to answer that, perhaps not, but they had taken their part in the "battle of Aberystwyth," a somewhat mysterious affair among the plum stalls in the market-place, possibly still remembered by men well advanced in years. In any case, we may be quite sure they would have acquitted themselves worthily if called upon, and they did indeed provide an inspiring note to all such ceremonial festivities. On this auspicious day of the opening of the line, to Mr. Ashford, the trumpeter of the Corps, fell the honour of sounding the first blast, and amidst the cheers of the countryside, some 600 ladies and gentlemen fell to dancing "to the music of the Montgomeryshire Yeomanry and Militia Bands, and the capital band of the Welshpool Cadet Corps, composed of the young gentlemen of Mr. Browne's academy."

And so, at long last, trains were to run through from Oswestry to Llanidloes. Six left Oswestry every weekday, the first timed to depart at 7 a.m., passing all the intermediate stations (including Arddleen, now added to the original five) to Welshpool without a stop, though this "express" was taken off the daily list some months later, and only ran on fair days. Four trains made the reverse journey from Llanidloes to Oswestry; while two trains ran each way on Sundays—a more generous service even than that afforded to-day! The Cambrian, as someone said, might still be a child, but it was a rapidly growing child. The guiding hand was at work, and additional limbs were shaping themselves, both at the Newtown and Oswestry end of the system, with such rapidity that we can best deal with them one by one.

The late MR. WILLIAM MICKLEBURGH, in the uniform of the Montgomeryshire Railway Volunteers.

The late CAPT. R. G. JEBB, of Ellesmere, a prominent promoter of the Oswestry and Whitchurch Railway and one of the first passengers to travel on the line.

CHAPTER V. FROM THE SEVERN TO THE SEA.

> "Wales is a land of mountains. Its mountains explain its isolation and its love of independence; they explain its internal divisions; they have determined, throughout its history, what the direction and method of its progress were to be."—THE LATE SIR O. M. EDWARDS.

I.

So far the lines already opened or under construction only traversed the valley of the Severn. It was now proposed to penetrate the uplands which lie between the banks of Sabrina and the shores of Cardigan Bay. It was a somewhat formidable undertaking. "The mountains of Carno," wrote the philosophic Pennant, "like the mountains of Gilboa, were celebrated for the fall of the mighty." On their steep slopes, in 1077 Gruffydd ab Cynan and Trahaiarn ab Caradoc had wrestled for the sovereignty of North Wales. Across their shoulders, some four centuries later, had marched the English troops of Henry IV. to their camp near Machynlleth, in a vain effort to subjugate the redoubtable Welsh chieftain, Owain Glyndwr. Now the mighty heads of the mountains were, at last, to shake and submit to the incursion of another invader, more insistent and more powerful than any that had gone before, and a Montgomeryshire engineer and contractor were to conquer where an English King had failed. In one respect only was their experience akin. Henry's army had become dissolved by the continuance of bad weather which gave them all cold feet. The rain, that falls alike upon the just and unjust, was to hamper Mr. David Davies's army of navvies, but never to deter them from reaching and abiding at Machynlleth.

In the initial stages of the new invasion all went well. So rapidly were the Parliamentary preliminaries negotiated that, on July 27th, 1857, while the promoters of the neighbouring Oswestry and Newtown Railway were still wrangling over their internecine rivalries, Royal Assent was given to the Newtown and Machynlleth Railway Bill, authorising the Company to raise a capital of £150,000 in £10 shares and loans to the extent of £50,000. The total length of the proposed line was 22½ miles and the works were to be completed within five years.

A month later the first ordinary meeting of the Company was held at Machynlleth. Sir Watkin presided over a most harmonious gathering, in striking contrast to some of the meetings which had assembled further east, and the directors in their report, read by Mr. D. Howell, who was to act as secretary until the amalgamation of the company in the Cambrian Railways in 1864, had little to say beyond offering congratulations to the shareholders on the speedy passing of their measure through Parliament. The report seems to have been adopted without comment, and the only other business was to appoint the board,—Earl Vane, Sir Watkin Williams Wynn, Mr. R. D. Jones, Mr. C. T. Thurston, Mr. J. Foulkes, Aberdovey, and Mr. L. Ruck. [54]

In a little over twelve months from that date the Company were in a position to begin operations. The contract had been let to Messrs. Davies and Savin (Mr. Benjamin Piercy again acting as engineer), and at the end of November, 1858, the first sod of the new link in the extended chain was turned amidst great popular rejoicings. So speedy had been the preparations that no time availed to procure a more ornamental implement, and the Countess Vane had to use an ordinary iron shovel for the purpose! A contemporary record gives the following account:—

"The Cutting of the First Sod was very properly fixed to take place at Machynlleth, not only out of compliment to the noble Earl and Countess Vane, but also to increase the interest of the inhabitants of this locality in the undertaking. The morning was ushered in by the bells of the parish church ringing out most musically, the firing of cannon, and similar demonstrations of good-will; and although in the early part of the morning the rain fell heavily, yet towards the time fixed for the proceedings to commence, bright Sol shone cheerfully over the beautiful hills and valleys of Montgomeryshire, and made everything look cheerful, as befitted the occasion. Two o'clock was the time fixed for cutting the first sod, but previously to this time a large procession was formed at the Town Hall, and proceeded to the ground in the following order:—

Band.

The Directors.

Flags and Banners.

The Demonstration Committee.

Flags and Banners.

The Shareholders, Visitors, and Well-wishers of the Company.

Contractors and Persons bearing the Barrow and Spade.

Flags and Banners.

The Children of the National and Vane Infant Schools.

Flags and Banners.

Band.

Miners and Quarrymen, headed by their Captains, all wearing Sashes.

Band.

First Friendly Society.

Flags and Banners.

Second Friendly Society.

Flags and Banners.

"On their arrival at the Schools the procession passed under a well-formed archway of evergreens and flowers, very massive in structure, over which were the mottoes,—'Success to the Newtown and Machynlleth Railway,' and 'Commercial and Agricultural prosperity.' At the entrance to the ground was another archway erected, over which was the motto—'Peace and Prosperity.' On reaching the spot where the ceremony was appointed to take place a large enclosure was railed out, at one end of which was a pavilion for the accommodation of the ladies, which was well filled. The parties had not long taken their allotted places before Lady Vane came upon the ground, and was welcomed in a way that must have been very gratifying to her, indeed it could not have been otherwise, for it is generally admitted that a kinder-hearted lady does not exist in the Principality, and she is most highly and deservedly popular, and well may Earl Vane be proud of possessing such a wife. She was accompanied by Lord Vane, and the young family, who appeared all thoroughly to enjoy the occasion."

The late EARL OF POWIS,
a prominent supporter of some of the earlier
Montgomeryshire Railway Schemes.

The late MR. DAVID HOWELL,
Secretary to the Newtown and Machynlleth
Railway Co. from its inauguration till its
amalgamation in the Consolidated Cambrian
Railways Co. in 1864.

After speeches by Lord and Lady Vane, her ladyship "having put on a pair of gauntlets, which were presented by the Committee of Management, proceeded to cut the first sod, which, having been deposited in the barrow presented by Messrs. Davies and Savin, the contractors, was wheeled to the end of the plank, after which Mrs. E. D. Jones, of Trafeign, performed the same ceremony, and was followed by Lord Seaham, and the other junior olive branches of the family. The bands played in their best style, and the cheering was most deafening, and thus ended this portion of the day's proceedings."

The subsequent proceedings were of a highly convivial nature, as befitted so auspicious an occasion. There was a generous imbibing of "a bountiful supply of Mr. Lloyd's prime port, sherry, etc.," and "a procession of miners and quarrymen, more than 100 of whom dined at the house of Mrs. Margaret Owen, the White Lion Inn, perhaps the most noted house in the county for the excellence of its ale."

The work on this line was of a rather different nature to that on which the contractors had been engaged on the Newtown and Llanidloes, and in bringing the Oswestry and Newtown line to completion. Instead of meandering, more or less, along river-side lowlands, the track had to be carried uphill and down-dale over the shoulder of the Montgomeryshire highlands, ascending to an altitude of 693 feet above sea level at Talerddig top by a climb of 273 feet from Caersws, and running down again by a 645 feet drop to the Dovey Valley at Machynlleth. This involved a gradient, at one point, of as much as 1 in 52, and, just after leaving the summit the line had to pierce through the hillside. A tunnel was originally thought of, but abandoned in favour of a cutting through solid rock to a depth of 120 feet. It was while excavations between the summit and the cutting were being made that the engineers discovered a strange geological formation, which, still observable from the train on the left-hand side immediately after leaving Talerddig station for Llanbrynmair, has come to be popularly known as "the natural arch." The work of excavating the cutting was no child's play. But it proved a profitable part of the contract, and it seems to have furnished not only enough stone for many of the adjacent railway works, but, according to popular rumour, the foundation of Mr. David Davies's vast fortune. Seeking an investment for the money he made out of it, it is said, Mr. Davies turned his thoughts to coal and in the rich mineral district of the Rhondda Valley it was sunk, rapidly to fructify, and to form the basis of that great industrial organisation the Ocean Collieries, famed throughout this country and wherever coal is used for navigation.

TALERDDIG CUTTING
Reproduced from the "Great Western Magazine"

For Mr. Davies was now left to finish the Newtown and Machynlleth line alone. While he was obtaining stone—and gold—out of Talerddig, his former partner, Mr. Savin, had turned his attention to another link in the chain between the Severn and the sea. In the end this arrangement, although it seems to have led to some little feeling between the former partners, which Mr. Whalley and others did their best to dispel, probably expedited the completion of the through connection. At any rate, it did not hinder progress among the hills. In this, the "long looked-for arrival of the world-wide famed iron-horse," as an expansive journalistic scribe put it, at Carno, was celebrated by rejoicings, and a dinner given by Mr. David Davies to his foremen and a presentation by him of a purse of £50 to the "meritorious engine-driver, Mr. Richard Metcalfe." Toasts were honoured, and Mr. Davies giving that of the evening, expatiated at length on the virtues of the redoubtable "Richard." The whole secret of the speed with which the railways he had constructed had been accomplished rested in "Richard's" zeal and prowess. Though the sea had covered their handiwork on the Vale of Clwyd railway half a dozen times, "Richard" had stuck to his post, by day and night—"from two o'clock on Monday morning till twelve o'clock on Saturday night, without once going to bed." If they had made nineteen miles of the Oswestry and Newtown track in thirteen months it was "in no small degree owing to 'Richard's' never-failing energy. He never grumbled, but always met me with a pleasant smile." No wonder that Carno shouted its three times three in "Richard's" honour and hardly less amazing that the good fellow, on rising to reply, utterly broke down and could not complete a sentence of his carefully prepared oration. "Never mind, 'Richard,'" exclaimed Mr. David Howell, "that is more eloquent than a speech."

From Carno, Metcalfe and his engine were soon to proceed to make the acquaintance of other friends and admirers further along the line. Llanbrynmair was soon to be reached, and another writer in the local Press is moved to compare its former remoteness, "verging close upon the classic 'Ultima Thule' of the first Roman," with the new conditions. "The railway," he says, "with its snorting, puffing and Vesuvian volumes of clouds, now to a certain extent breaks upon the whilom monotony of this valley among mountains; its aptly termed iron-horse (Mars-like, but still in a placable mood) rolls majestically along, conveying the very backbone of creation from the granite rock, ready trimmed, and requiring but the cunning hand of the workman to fix the stones in their appropriate place to span the meandering Jaen and Twymyn streams."

One of the bridges across the Twymyn, indeed, skilfully designed by Mr. Piercy, with whom was associated Mr. George Owen, was a notable structure. It consisted of three arches, its extreme height, 70 feet above the rushing waters of this mountain torrent, the abutments being large blocks of Talerddig stone and the arches turned in best Ruabon brick. For, continues our chronicler, it was a highly satisfactory fact for Welsh patriots to contemplate that Mr. Davies was "working his line by means of Welsh materials, drawn from inexhaustible Welsh mountains, his workmen are natives, the planning and workmanship is also native, and he himself a thorough and spirited Welshman."

Less placable were some of the influences which began to exert themselves further afield. The Board having set their hand to a proposed agreement by which the Great Western Company undertook to work the line for 40 per cent. of the gross earnings and an exchange of traffic arrangement, it became the signal for raising again the old bogey of rival "interests." An anonymous writer in the "Open Column" of the "Oswestry Advertiser," describing the Newtown and Machynlleth as "the worst managed railway in the course of formation," warned Machynlleth against its impending doom. It would mean a break of journey at Newtown, and, to avert this, the North Western, once the personification of all unrighteousness, was now transformed into the fairy godmother, who, by pressing forward its co-operation with the Bishop's Castle, Mid-Wales and Manchester and Milford undertakings, was urged to carry forward connecting links from Llanidloes over the shoulder of Plynlimmon, as a competitive route to the sea. The article attracted some attention at the next meeting of the Newtown and Machynlleth shareholders, where the bargain with the Great Western was warmly defended, both by Capt. R. D. Pryce, who presided, and by Mr. David Davies, as the largest shareholder as well as contractor. But the Oswestrian alarm was groundless. What looked a rosy prospect from the Newtown and Machynlleth Company's point of view, had another aspect, when it came to be more fully considered at Paddington, and, in spite of repeated reminders, that Company failed to take the necessary steps to secure its ratification by its shareholders, and the working agreement for the new line was transferred to the Oswestry and Newtown, who were already working the Newtown and Llanidloes Railway. The incipient Cambrian, in fact, willy nilly, was now beginning to experience the sensation which comes, sooner or later, to healthily expanding youth, when it has to stand alone. Tumbles there might be ahead, but the day of leading strings was finally left behind.

Two engines "of a powerful class" with 4ft. 6in. wheels, capable of hauling 140 ton loads up 1/52 gradients at 15 miles an hour, accelerated to 25 miles on the easier levels had been quoted for by Messrs. Sharp, Stewart and Co., of the Atlas Works, Manchester, in 1861, at the cost of £2,445 each, and by the end of 1862 the Company were fully equipped to cope with the traffic of the district.

At the end of the first week of the new year (1863) the opening ceremony took place. The engines, "Countess Vane" and "Talerddig," drew a train of 1,500 passengers, who had marched in procession to the Machynlleth Station, up the long incline, over the Talerddig summit and down to Newtown and back. At the intermediate stations, Cemmes Road, Llanbrynmair, Carno, Pontdolgoch and Caersws, it was hailed with vociferous applause as it sped on its way, and as Newtown was approached the travellers found themselves passing under triumphal arches, to the clang of church bells and the blare of bands. On the leading engine rode the young Marquis of Blandford playing "See the Conquering Here Comes" on the cornet-a-piston, Mr. George Owen, Mr. Davies and Mr. Webb. Earl Vane was in the train and received a public welcome at the station. Then the inevitable speeches. The return train was still longer and took two hours to reach Machynlleth, where the jubilations were renewed, and

Countess Vane, to whom Mr. Davies presented a silver spade in honour of the previous ceremony of sod cutting, declared the line open. More speeches, luncheon, toasts and processioning ab lib and "so home."

The time, however, had come for a memorable parting. From the consummation of this project Mr. David Davies's connection with the Cambrian, as one of its contractors, was to cease. He had saved it from early death, and guided the infant through its difficult teething time, while at the same time he was employed in building other railways, which, later, were to become closely linked with its fuller life. Among these was the Mid-Wales, to become amalgamated with the Cambrian in 1904, the Brecon and Merthyr, over four miles of whose metals, from Talyllyn Junction to Brecon, Cambrian trains were from that date to run, and the Manchester and Milford, which formed a junction with the Cambrian at Aberystwyth. But so far as the Cambrian itself is concerned Mr. Davies's future association was to be that of a director, an office, in its turn, dramatically terminated amidst fresh thunder clouds which had not yet appeared above the horizon.

II.

Mr. Savin, as we have seen, had, during these later stages of progress with the making of the line from Newtown, been busily engaged still nearer the coast. A company with an ambitious name and a not less ambitious aim had been formed to build a railway from Aberystwyth to Machynlleth and along the shores of Merionethshire to Portmadoc, the port of shipment of the Festiniog slate traffic, and eventually to continue, through Pwllheli to that wonderful prospective harbour, upon which the eyes of railway promoters had already been turned without avail, Porthdynlleyn, near Nevin. [63] Its close connection with the other local undertakings is shown by the agreement under which the Oswestry and Newtown was to subscribe £75,000, and the Newtown and Llanidloes £25,000 by the creation of 5 per cent. preference stock, a sum ultimately increased in the case of the former Company by another £100,000.

Borne on the wings of Mr. Whalley's eloquence, Aberystwyth, assembled in public meeting, led by the Mayor, Mr. Robert Edwards, gave its enthusiastic support to the scheme. This was followed by another meeting, at which Mr. Piercy, as engineer, outlined the plan and bade the inhabitants look forward to the day when the railway was to enable them to compete with successful rivals on the North Wales Coast, and once more justify for them the proud name of "the Brighton of Wales." Other railway companies were inclined to be obstructive, but their opposition was not altogether formidable, and when Mr. Abraham Howell appeared in the role of mediator between conflicting interests, the way was soon prepared for proceeding apace with the scheme. So harmonious, indeed, had the atmosphere become that within less than two months of this meeting the Company's Bill had received Royal Assent, almost a record, surely, in those days of interminable controversy! Mr. Savin's project was to begin by carrying the line, whence it linked up with the Newtown and Machynlleth at the latter place, as far as Ynyslas. Here, at the nearest point on the seaboard, the mists which hang over the great bogs that stretch from the sand-dunes up to the foothills of Plynlimmon, took fantastic shape in the eye of the ambitious contractor. He may, perchance, have heard the story told of a man who owned a barren piece of land bordering the seashore. A friend advised him to convert it to some use. The owner replied that it would not grow grass, or produce corn, was unfit for fruit trees, and could not even be converted into an ornamental lake as the soil was too sandy to retain the water. "Then," said the friend, "why not make it a first-class watering place?" This, at any rate, was the project on which Mr. Savin set his heart. But not even first-class watering places can be built in a day, and the contractor made a modest beginning with a row of lodging houses. Alas! not for the last time, the parable of the man who built upon the sands was to have its application to these Welsh coast undertakings. The houses were no sooner finished than they began to sink, and some time later they were pulled down and the material put to more hopeful and profitable use.

Latest Cambrian Passenger Express Engine.

Ynyslas remains to-day a lonely swamp, but somewhat better luck attended the effort to carry the excursionist on to Borth. The line was pushed on there, and an old farm house, on the outskirts of what was then nothing but a tiny fishing village, was converted into a station. The following July the line was open for traffic. Curiously enough, little public interest seems to have been aroused in Borth itself by the event. The inhabitants of the village were mainly engaged in seafaring, and the arrival of the steam engine, in the opinion of some, boded no good. As for English visitors— what use were they? The story, indeed, is told that some four enterprising tourists, who had arrived ahead of the railway, sought accommodation in vain in the village, and had perforce to make the best of it in a contractor's railway wagon that stood on a siding of the unfinished line. They cuddled up under a tarpaulin sheet and settled down for the night, when someone gave the wagon a shove and starting down an incline on the unballasted track it proceeded merrily on its way to Ynyslas. Not so merry the affrighted and unwilling passengers, who, when day broke, discovered themselves marooned in a remote spot miles from anywhere productive of breakfast bacon and eggs!

But, if Borth itself looked on askance, Aberystwyth was ready enough to acclaim the approach of the railway. The resort on the Rheidol had already begun to attract visitors who completed the journey from Llanidloes or Machynlleth by coach, and now there was the prospect, in the early future, of the railway running into the town itself. So, very early on the day when the first train was to steam into and out of Borth, vehicles of all sorts crowded the road from Aberystwyth, the narrow street of Borth was rapidly thronged with an excited multitude who flowed over on the sands. At 8-30 a.m. the train left, with 100 excursionists. It was followed by another at 1 p.m., for which 530 took tickets. There was a great scramble for seats, and every one of the thirty coaches of which the train was composed, was packed to the doors. Those who failed to obtain a footing formed an avenue a mile long through which the train moved out amidst tumultuous applause. In the carriages the passengers shouted, talked, ate, drank and—sang hymns! The twelve miles to Machynlleth took about twenty-five minutes to accomplish, and, arrived there, the excursionists enjoyed themselves immensely, "as," says a contemporary recorder, "Aberystwyth people generally manage to do when from home at any rate."

Nor were the good folks of Aberystwyth peculiar in their joy. A Shropshire newspaper published a leading article of a column and a half descriptive of "six hours by the seaside for half-a-crown,"—the return excursion fare from Shrewsbury and Oswestry, while Poolonians could travel for a florin. The result was a mighty rush of trippers, not the less attracted, possibly, by the additional announcement that the railway company had thoughtfully opened a refreshment room at Borth station! So great, indeed, was the press of traffic, that the company's servants sometimes had considerable difficulty in coping with it. One day all the tickets were exhausted, but the stationmaster at Carno, one Burke, an Irishman, not to be beaten, booked some thirty or forty farm labourers with "cattle tickets." The manager passed next day and remonstrated. "Why, Burke," said he, "the men won't like your making beasts of them!" "Och, yure honour," returned the stationmaster, "many of them made bastes of themselves before they returned."

Indeed, the scenes at Borth on the arrival of these excursions were occasionally almost indescribable. One scribe invokes the loan of the pencil of Hogarth adequately to portray it. "From a cover of stones close by springs an urchin lithe and swift; another and another, ten, twelve or more, 'naked as unto earth they came,' and away in single file across the beach into the sea. The vans move ponderously on, pushed by mermen and mermaids, and out spring any quantity of live Hercules. Very curious must be the sight, if one might judge by the crowds of ladies—well women at any rate—and gentlemen around every group of bathers. Boats are in great request and the ladies cling very lovingly to the boatmen who, in return, hug them tightly as they embark or disembark their fair freight. The very porpoises, gambling out there, seem to enjoy the whole thing heartily and shake their fat sides at the fun. Our friend with the hammer discourses learnedly about those long ridges of hard rock which stand out over the Dovey Plain when, gracious me! we look round and, will you believe it? There was a bevy of females in a state of—shall I go on? No; but I will just say we saw them waddling like ducks into the water. The porpoises were alarmed and betook themselves off. And so did we. Had the bathers been black instead of white we should have thought ourselves on the coast of Africa. Such an Adam and Eve-ish state of things we never saw before. Well, honi soit qui mal y pense."

Anyhow, thus did the six hours swiftly pass in those unregenerate days. For Mr. Savin had yet to build his Borth hotel and lodging houses, which to-day give welcome shelter to a very different throng of visitors, summer after summer, attracted by the placid beauties and the invigorating air of Cardigan Bay. It was, at worst, but a temporary orgy, marking, as it were, a new epoch in the life of the Cambrian; whose lengthening limbs now stretched from the Severn to the sea.

CHAPTER VI. THE BATTLE OF ELLESMERE.

"The question of a railway is now or never."—THE LATE MR. R. G. JEBB, of Ellesmere.

No period, since the wild days of the "railway mania," was more pregnant of schemes than the later months of 1860. They sprang up like mushrooms all along the Shropshire border, and some of them, like mushrooms, as suddenly suffered decay. A facetious Salopian prophet ventured publicly to predict that "we shall hear next of a railway to Llansilin (a remote village among the border hills) or the moon." His ratiocination was hardly exaggerated. A "preliminary prospectus" was actually published for carrying a railway, at a cost of under £10,000 per mile, from Shrewsbury, through Kinnerley and Porthywaen, thence "near Llanfyllin and Llanrhaiadr," to Llangynog, "through the Berwyn hills" to Llandrillo, and so to Dolgelley and Portmadoc. It was to be worked and maintained by the West Midland, Shrewsbury and Coast of Wales Railway Co.; the prospects of mineral and passenger traffic were "most promising," and throughout its entire length of 90 miles, the promoters pointed out with all the emphasis which italics can afford, "it has only one tunnel, and that slightly exceeding a mile and half in length." Eventually, a line, partly following this route, under the less comprehensive title of the West Shropshire Mineral Railway, and later known as "the Potteries," constructed from a station in Abbey Forgate, Shrewsbury, to Llanymynech, and on to Nantmawr, with a branch from Kinnerley to Criggion, ran for a time, then fell into abeyance and disrepair, and was in recent years re-opened under the Light Railways Act as the Shropshire and Montgomeryshire Railway, an independent company.

But, in its original form, the undertaking was apparently to be no friendly competitor with the existing Oswestry and Newtown and associated lines, whose ambition it had, for some time, been to extend its northern terminus, resting on the Great Western branch at Oswestry, through Ellesmere to Whitchurch, there to form a more serviceable junction with the London and North Western from Shrewsbury to Crewe, and the busy hives of Lancashire. But more formidable opposition was already afoot elsewhere. The Great Western, none too eager, as we have seen, to assist independent undertakings in Montgomeryshire, were ready enough to capture traffic in other quarters, and their answer to the Oswestry and Whitchurch project was to formulate a scheme for a branch from Rednal to Ellesmere, with incidental hints about constructing a loop to place Oswestry on their main line. Draughtsmen were busy everywhere with pens and plans. Public halls echoed to the optimistic eloquence of promoters and counter promoters, and powder and shot was being hurriedly got together for the tremendous fusilade in the Parliamentary committee rooms, where, for many a long day, there was to rage and sway the battle for the rights and privileges of bringing the steam engine into the little town of Ellesmere.

For, though wider schemes were involved in the struggle, Ellesmere was the pivot on which arguments and contentions centred. In such a conflict, needless to say, all the old rivalries of "leviathan" interests, of which we have already heard so much, re-emerged. What was still called the "Montgomeryshire party"—the men who had brought the other local railways into existence in spite of well-nigh overwhelming difficulties—continued to look for association with the North Western for greater salvation. Others favoured the chance of obtaining increased facilities for through traffic from the Great Western. Between the two warring elements, Ellesmere itself, as one of its most estimable and influential citizens had put it, believed it was "now or never" for them. In the Parliamentary Committee Rooms, where the evidence occupied thirteen days, and counsels' speeches several more, the two projects were stubbornly fought out. Great Western witnesses came forward to aver that, owing to the haste with which the Shrewsbury and Chester Railway had been projected, Oswestry had been left too much in the lurch, and the time was now come for reconsideration of its claims to be brought on to the main line. Mr. Sergeant Wheeler, with all the command of forensic eloquence, drew visions of the Shropshire market town as "a great central place of meeting for the people all round." All that was necessary was to build a line from Oswestry to Rednal, and then the projected branch from Rednal to Ellesmere, and Rednal itself might become a second Rugby or Crewe; who could tell? As to the continuation of such a line from Ellesmere to Whitchurch, true, Paddington was not enthusiastic, but when they found that that was the price demanded for any measure of local support, they were ready to pay it.

In Oswestry there was, naturally enough, a general approval of any step which would place the town on the Great Western main line, and no small point was made of the fact that it would be better to have one station than two. Moreover, Mr. R. J. Croxon. whose words were weighted with the influence of a family solicitor, private banker and town clerk, was of opinion that, apart from anything else, to carry a line, as Mr. Whalley proposed, for two miles by the side of the turnpike to Whittington would be "very dangerous to people driving along," and the attention of the Trustees ought to be called to it. But, unfortunately for Mr. Croxon and those who shared his fears in this regard, it was the business of the local surveyor to examine the plans, and he was "engaged on the other side."

Thus even among Oswestrians was opinion divided between the rival routes, and men like Alderman Thomas Minshall and Alderman Peploe Cartwright, who had stood shoulder to shoulder in the fight for independent interests in the making of the Oswestry and Newtown Railway, were now inclined to regard each others' sympathies with some suspicion.

Further down the proposed line the weight was thrown rather more decisively in favour of the Whalley scheme. Whitchurch had petitioned against the Great Western proposals, though Captain Cust, who gave evidence for the larger company, was moved to dismiss this effort as the work of "Captain Clement Hill and lot of ragamuffins." Attempts were even made to disparage the local undertaking by reference to Mr. Savin, who had agreed to carry out the line on similar terms of lease already adopted elsewhere, as a "haberdasher, not in a position to subscribe millions towards railway projects." In Ellesmere the argument that the Great Western scheme would bring the agricultural area into close touch with the North Wales coalfields was quickly answered by the counter-plea that the independent company could also build a branch from that spot to Ruabon or Wrexham, and powers to that effect "would be applied for as soon as what may be called the main line from Oswestry to Whitchurch was carried." Even the larger landowners through whose estates the rival engineers had marched with their instruments differed in their point of approach. Sir John Kynaston, Bart., of Hardwicke, near Ellesmere, who, as someone said, "if he had been left alone, was willing, like Marcus Curtius, to sacrifice himself for the public good, was brought and instructed to give evidence about embankments," one of which, on Mr. Whalley's line, by the way, it was supposed (though in error) would shut out his view of the Vale of Llangollen, and "destroy the happiness of his existence for the remainder of his days." Sir John Hanmer, Bart., M.P., on the other hand, was inclined to become rhapsodic. He looked upon a railway "as a fine work of art," which any painter might be glad to include in his landscape—only, of course, it must not cut off a landed proprietor from his woods and his other wild grounds, as the Great Western scheme proposed to do, and against this he not only objected but petitioned.

In the end the Committee declared the preamble of the Montgomeryshire party, for their Oswestry, Ellesmere, and Whitchurch Railway to be proved, and that of the Great Western not proved, though the Chairman regretted to add that the finding was not unanimous. In the lobbies rumour had it that it was, in fact, only arrived at by the casting vote of that gentleman himself. Be that as it may, it sufficed. Once again "independent" effort, astutely engineered, had triumphed over the all-powerful interests of a great and wealthy company, and amongst those who had hoped and feared and hoped again for the success of the Oswestry Ellesmere and Whitchurch scheme enthusiasm knew no bounds.

In Ellesmere a great and excited crowd awaited news from London at the Bridgewater Hotel. They watched for the omnibus from Gobowen, which it was expected might bear the fateful tidings. But either the omnibus failed to arrive, or, if it did, it had no intelligence to impart. Shortly afterwards, however, a special messenger came post haste along the road from Oswestry, and in a moment the news flashed through the little town. "Victory"! An attempt was made to ring the bells, but the churchwarden could not be found, and no one else had authority to pull the ropes. So that the concourse fell back on the time-honoured procession, and led by a drum and fife band, and headed by the Bailiffs, the cheering throng paraded the streets while cannon booming from the market place startled the countryside for a mile or more around. Oswestry, assembled in public meeting, put to flight its town clerk's gloomy prognostications with hilarious speeches, and outside the more dignified civic circles popular demonstration took still more picturesque form.

The return of a number of witnesses who had gone up to London to give evidence against the local scheme and in support of the Great Western was awaited at the Oswestry station by a hostile crowd. Some delay in their arrival home was occasioned by an untoward incident even before they finally left London. Seating themselves in a first-class compartment in the rear of the train at Paddington, they waited at first patiently and then impatiently for it to start. At last, unable to understand the delay, one of them put out his head and asked a passing official when the train was going. "It has gone" was the laconic reply. The coach which they had chosen was not attached to the rest of the train, and they were not so meticulously careful about examining tickets on the Great Western system as they are to-day. When the belated passengers did eventually reach Oswestry, the crowd was still there. What was more, they had had time to organise what was deemed a suitable reception. Among the witnesses was a gentleman who, it appeared, had at one time been very short of pence, and, it was alleged, had left his abode without paying the rent. Somehow or another this little fact had been raked up and a number of wags had cut the shape of a latch-key out of a sheet of tin. As he alighted from the train this was dangled before him at the end of a long pole, with a pendant inscription, "Who left the key under the door?"

The promoters of the new undertaking, of which Mr. George Lewis became first secretary, with offices in Oswald Chambers, Oswestry, had every reason for satisfaction. Royal assent was given to their Bill in August, 1861, authorising a capital of £150,000 in £10 shares, with £50,000 on loan, the work to be completed within five years. There were, however, still tough battles to be waged over subsequent efforts to obtain sanction for certain deviations and extensions, against which the Great Western continued to fight tooth and nail with a counter-offensive of their own. No fewer than three distinct schemes were now before the public, with all sorts of loops and junctions at Rednal or Mile End, near Whittington, and branches from Bettisfield to Wem, or to Yorton, and from Ellesmere to Ruabon. But it is an easier task to draw plans on a map than to carry them out. The Wem branch never matured, the link with Denbighshire only after many years, and then to Wrexham and not Ruabon. So far as the main issue was concerned, however, the Great Western again failed to prove their preamble, and another signal was given for local rejoicings over the result. Not only at Oswestry and Ellesmere and other places along the route of the new line, but as far afield as Montgomery and Llanfyllin, where a branch line of their own was being promoted to Llanymynech, hats were thrown into the air and healths were drunk to the victory for local enterprise. Oswestry parish church bells rang for two days, and the Rifle Corps band blew itself dry outside the houses of Mr. Savin, Mr. George Owen and others. Mr. Savin himself, returning from London, during these proceedings, met "with a reception at Oswestry such as no man ever received before." Carried shoulder high through the streets of the town, accompanied by a surging throng of cheering admirers, armed with torches, to the tune of "See the Conquering Hero comes," he was addressed in congratulatory vein by several of his fellow-citizens, and it was only when a first and second attempt to fly from the embarrassment of so tumultuous a welcome had failed, that he succeeded, on a third, in making his escape. The "small haberdasher," who had been deemed incapable of organising railway schemes, had indeed become something very like a railway king!

But we are anticipating events. At the end of August, 1861, the first sod had been cut at Ellesmere, where it was proposed to begin the construction, proceeding first in the direction of Whitchurch. The ceremony was performed by Sir John Hanmer and Mr. John Stanton, in a field belonging to Mr. W. A. Provis, "not far from the workhouse," and a spade and barrow, suitably inscribed, was presented to Sir John by Messrs. Savin and Ward, the contractors. There was the usual ceremonial, inclusive of banqueting and speech-making, and banners, emblazoned with such appropriate mottoes as "Whalley for ever," "Hurrah for Sir John Hanmer and John Stanton, Esquire," floated in the breeze. One ingenious gentleman, elaborating the topical theme, had erected a flag which, we are told, "attracted special attention from its significance and quaintness," representing a donkey cart with two passengers on one side and a steam engine and carriages on the other, to personify "Ellesmere of yesterday," and "Ellesmere of to-day," with the philosophic addendum, "Evil communications corrupt good manners," "Aye, says the preacher, every valley shall be raised and every hill shall be brought low." "Aye, says the teacher, let us bless the bridge that carries us safely over," "Aye, aye, quoth honest nature." The application to evil communications might, in such a connection, be a little ambiguous, but presumably nobody imagined it to refer to the Oswestry, Ellesmere and Whitchurch Railway!

The allusion to bridges was rather more germane; for, in building the line towards Whitchurch, which was the first section taken in hand, the engineers were faced with a bridging problem of a peculiar nature, and only less in magnitude than that which had confronted the constructors of the famous Liverpool and Manchester Railway thirty years earlier. Partly in order to avoid interfering with Sir John Hanmer's property, and partly because they deemed it the better way, the engineers decided to carry the line over Whixall Moss, a wide area of bog land lying between Bettisfield and Fenns Bank. This, it was supposed, might even be drained by making the railway across its quivering surface, but hopes of this sort were not to be realised, for it remains to-day a wild, but picturesque stretch of heather and silver birches, where the peat-digger plies his trade with, perhaps, as much profit as the farmer would in tilling it. But as to its power to bear the weight of passing trains the engineers had little doubt. The canal already crossed it, and though in making soundings the surveyors once lost their 35 foot rod in the morass, this, was near the canal bank, and it did not deter them in their efforts to discover a means of securing the railway from similar disaster. The average depth of the moss was found to be twelve feet, but there were areas where it was only nine feet deep, and at most 17 feet, and when the bottom was reached it was discovered to be sand.

So, proceeding merrily, Mr. George Owen first drained the site of the line by means of deep side and lateral drains filled with brushwood and grig. He then laid strong faggots three feet thick and from eight to twelve feet long, and over these placed a framework of larch poles extending the entire width of the rails. The poles were then interlaced with branches of hazel and brushwood and upon this the sleepers and rails were laid, the whole being ballasted with sand and other light material. And, in the end it proved a triumph for courage and ingenuity. Though there might be some slight oscillation, heavy trains have been running over this interesting two or three mile stretch for many a long year without the slightest mishap.

Not to be outdone by little Ellesmere, another "first sod" was turned at Oswestry on September 4th, 1862, by Miss Kinchant of Park Hall, and Miss Lloyd, daughter of the Mayor of the borough, on the Shelf Bank field, hard by the existing terminus of the Oswestry and Newtown Railway, with which the new line was to be connected. The streets were in gala dress, and while the leading citizens fared sumptuously on the Wynnstay Arms bowling green, and disported themselves at a "rural fête," tea was served to "the poorer women of the town and neighbourhood." In addition to the residents many came from Ellesmere in wagons drawn by a decorated traction engine,—significant emblem of the new power which was shortly to bring the two neighbouring and ever friendly places within a quarter of an hour's distance of each other.

Work now went ahead on both sections of the line, under the personal supervision of Messrs. Thomas and John Savin and Mr. John Ward, and by the spring of 1863 the railway was ready for traffic over the eleven miles between Ellesmere and Whitchurch. The honour of being the first passengers to make the journey belongs, appropriately enough, to the late Capt. Jebb and his company of Rifles, who, by courtesy of the contractors, were driven to Whitchurch on April 20th, a few other friends accompanying them. The official trial trip was made shortly after, in a train drawn by "two heavy engines," the "Montgomery" and the "Hero," and in crossing Whixall Moss, we are told, "the deflection was almost inappreciable." Captain Tyler was now able to pass the line as entirely satisfactory, and, early in the morning on the first Monday in May, a little group of Ellesmerians assembled at their new station to witness the first regular train leave for Whitchurch. No doubt their hearts swelled with pride, but beyond the usual exhibition of such emotion as so notable an event inspired, there was no public acclaim.

Another twelve months were to elapse before the remaining section, from Ellesmere to Oswestry, was ready for traffic. In July 1864, however, this link was forged, and the event synchronizing with the completion of the work at the other end of the chain, from Borth to Aberystwyth, it threw open the whole length of what was about to become, under the Consolidation Act, the main line of the Cambrian Railways.

CHAPTER VII. THE COAST SECTION.

> "When they saw the Crimean Campaign they seemed about to be engaged in against the sea, he thought it had been very much to the advantage of the Welsh Coast line, if, on the formation of the Board the Directors had been put through a series of questions in early English history, and if their engineer had been directed to report to them on the maritime events of the reign of Canute."—
> EDWARD, THIRD EARL OF POWIS.

No Chapter in the story of the Cambrian is more intimately touched with the spirit of romance, none more prolific of pathetic humour, than that which concerns what is to-day termed the Coast Section. For the moment, however, all was sunshine and success. The continuation of the line from Borth to Aberystwyth was completed for traffic, as we have just seen, in the summer of 1864, and on that auspicious day when trains began to run through from Whitchurch to the new terminus on the banks of the Rheidol the rejoicings in Aberystwyth were such as to eclipse even those who had marked earlier stages of the construction of the various railways now linked in one long chain. Indeed, the triumphal procession which made its way to the coast was bent on more than one celebration. The day was also to mark the opening of the hotel which Mr. Savin had built at Borth, and when the train finally arrived at Aberystwyth at a quarter past three it was accorded a civic welcome; the Mayor, Mr. Morgan, and Corporation tendering to Messrs. Thomas and John Savin an address, in which thanks were poured out upon these "benefactors" to the locality. A move was then made to the promenade, where Mrs. Edwards drove the first pile in the new pier, and, after much processioning, the great assembly sat down at the Belle Vue Hotel for a banquet of which, surely, the like has never been seen in the town since! Here his Worship, supported by Earl Vane, Capt. E. L. Pryse, M.P., Mr. Thomas Barnes, M.P., Capt. R. D. Pryce, the Contractors, Engineers, and many other ardent workers for or well-wishers of the undertaking, presided over a flow of oratory, the report of which occupied over five columns of the newspapers, and visions of a new Aberystwyth swam before the eyes of the guests, wonderful and beatific! Such, indeed, was the sumptuousness of the repast, and the wealth of oratory, that it was eleven at night before the company could be persuaded to take their places in the return train, and at three o'clock the next morning a jovial party arrived home at Oswestry, tired and sleepy, though happy and glorious.

But the "Crimean campaign" of girdling the coast of Merionethshire and penetrating onward to the distant peninsula of Lleyn, which was part of the Aberystwyth and Welsh Coast scheme, was yet only in its earlier stages, and already the difficulties of the undertaking had had their sobering effects. The original idea of Mr. Piercy was to build a huge bridge from Ynyslas across the estuary of the Dovey to Aberdovey, whence it was proposed to run a service of steam boats to Ireland. Work was begun with seeking a foundation in the shifting sands. Men were engaged with the boring rods, but they could only labour at low tide, and in the long intervals when the water was high, adjacent hostelries afforded a too attractive method of spending enforced leisure, so that often, it is said, when the waters had receded enough to renew operations, some of the borers were too bemused to know whether they were on the solid earth or not. At any rate, no sure foundation could be found, either by Philip drunk or by Philip sober, and it was reluctantly concluded that another means of bridging the gulf must be sought.

Adopting the wise Tennysonian counsel, the promoters eventually decided to "take the bend," and Parliamentary power was sought for this deviation of the original scheme. It was opposed by the Great Western Railway as inimical to their project of carrying a line from Bala to Barmouth and so forming a connection with the Welsh Coast, and their antagonism was only disposed of after a compromise had been made in the Parliamentary Committee Room, by which the great company obtained power to build the bridge themselves, if they wished, within ten years, and the tolls on the deviation were to be charged only for the same distance as if the traffic had been carried by the bridge. So the line was carried round to cross the Dovey at a narrow point near Glandyfi and connect the coast line with the other railway there.

Hence the existence of, perhaps, the most beautifully situated of all railway stations, formerly called Glandovey Junction, but changed in recent years to Dovey Junction to avoid confusion with the adjacent Glandovey station, at the same time transformed into Glandyfi. Being only intended for changing trains the station is peculiar in having no exit, and the very few passengers who ever alight here for other purposes than entering another train have, presumably to make their way as best they can along the line. Another feature of this station is that its buildings and adjuncts lie in three counties. The station itself is in Montgomeryshire. The stationmaster's house, just over the river bridge is in Merioneth, and from the signalbox the signalman works an up distant signal which is planted in the soil of Cardiganshire!

But this connection only came later, in August 1867, when the six miles of line from Aberdovey to the Junction was carried along the estuary shore and through the four tunnels which, until the Mid-Wales Railway was absorbed in 1904, remained the only ones on the whole system. For a considerable time after the coast line was opened passengers were carried from Aberdovey by ferry to Ynyslas. At high tide the boat could make for the station, but when the water was low it berthed on the Cardiganshire side, at a lower landing place, whence travellers and baggage proceeded by a little branch into Ynyslas station.

The first sod on the Merionethshire side had been cut, in April 1862, by Mrs. Foulkes of Aberdovey, on the Green near the Corbett Arms Hotel at Towyn, without formal ceremony, but in the presence of Mr. Piercy and Mr. Savin, and "a few scores of persons who cheered lustily." We may hope that even this mild demonstration did something to hearten the promoters in their herculean task. For several miles along the shore the line had to be protected against the assault of the high tides that periodically sweep Cardigan Bay, and it was soon only too evident that ordinary ramparts were no sure buttress against Atlantic rollers. More than once the permanent way was washed by the waves and engineer and contractor, viewing the dismal wreckage, must have felt that noble references to the moral of Canute, however pungent, were not altogether inapropos.

There were toilers at this work, however, who had never heard of the Danish King and bode not of what the maritime history of England might teach. To them the arrival of the first trial train on the banks of the Dysynni was more pertinently an occasion for "celebration," and sixty pounds being quickly collected for the purpose, and as quickly spent, rumour has it that, alas! the festivities ended for some in a few reflective hours, we may hope profitably, if not too comfortably, spent in the local lock-up.

But even when the Dysynni had been safely bridged,—not without anxious days when piles refused to become embedded in the shingly bed of the river—the troubles of the constructors were far from concluded. Beyond Llwyngwril, to which the line was opened for traffic in November, 1863,— the engines and coaches had been brought by barge across the Dovey from Ynyslas—there lay a still more formidable barrier to rapid progress. For the cliffs hereabouts, which, with their steep declivity down to the rock-strewn shore, left scarcely a foothold for the wandering mountain sheep, were enough to daunt the heart of any but the most courageous and determined engineer. Here, again, the problem rose as to whether they should be tunnelled or the line carried along their sloping edge, supported by sea-walls, as was the high road above. But the high road itself shaved the edge of the precipice so closely that, it is related, in the old coaching days, many people preferred leaving the vehicle at the top of the hill to swinging down such a slope. Eventually choice fell on the latter alternative, sailors being employed to assist in the work by reason of their greater experience on such seagirt ledges! It was, indeed, a hazardous venture; for the extreme narrowness of the ground to work upon, sometimes tapering away to practically no ground at all, hampered the task at every step, and the difficulty of building a track along which heavy trains could run at high speed was never quite surmounted. Even to-day trains descending the 1 in 60 decline are carefully regulated in speed, no bad arrangement, after all, since this stretch of line commands, on a clear day, one of the finest peeps of the whole charming panorama of scenery along the coast of North Wales.

But engineer and contractor had something better to do than admire the view. Below them and beyond, even when Barmouth Junction was reached in July, 1865, there lay another obstacle which could not be avoided by any but the widest detour. Trains could, and were eventually carried around the narrow neck of the Dovey; they must cross the estuary of the Mawddach almost at its widest point in order to gain the Barmouth shore. Meanwhile, the line was carried along the southern bank of the river, by what is now the Dolgelley branch, to Penmaenpool, and the public had to remain content with such facilities as this localised service could provide.

And a wonderful service it appears to have been! Old inhabitants still tell tales of how goods trains would pull up at remote wayside spots while driver and guard went trapping hares that made good prices in the neighbouring markets, where no inconvenient questions were asked concerning their capture. Or it might be that, now and again, a waggon load of beer barrels was consigned to some village inn. It was then the business of those in charge so to marshal the train that the "stuff" was placed in convenient proximity to the engine, and, in the seclusion of some cutting, a halt would be made for some mysterious reason. To clamber over the tender into the adjacent waggon was a simple matter. Still simpler, in expert hands, was the process of forcing up the hoop of one of the barrels, tapping it and drawing it till the engine bucket foamed alluringly, then plugging it up again, and drawing back the hoop into its original position. On delivery the consignee might complain of short weight, but that it was a question for the brewer and the company to settle as best they could. None of the running staff knew anything about it; and, as for the lateness of the train, well, was any train ever punctual in those days, and who bothered about half an hour's delay?

Besides, there was something more important to bother about. Actions in Chancery had begun to distract the attention of worried directors, and these retarded progress with the construction of the line. So it was not until June 1869 that the Cambrian continued beyond Penmaenpool, and, even when

Dolgelley was eventually approached, passengers had to alight at a platform some little distance from the town. Only when the Great Western Railway from Ruabon was completed did the trains from Barmouth Junction run into Dolgelley station proper.

Many and difficult as were the engineering problems involved in the construction of the coast line none aroused greater interest or put scientific skill and courage to a severer test than that, to which we have already briefly alluded, of carrying the railway over the sand and river current into Barmouth. To the lay mind it appeared an almost insuperable task, and there were those who did not hesitate to whisper their doubts as to its practicability, one well-known local gentleman being reported to have gone as far as publicly to undertake to eat the first engine which ever crossed that formidable gulf. But engineers and craftsmen set to work with a will, and before long what had appeared an impossibility was rapidly taking shape as an actuality. Eight hundred yards in length, the greater portion was constructed on timber piles, over 500 in number, in 113 spans, driven into the sand. The navigable channel, at the Barmouth end, was crossed by an iron-work construction, of seven fixed and one opening span. The latter was of the drawbridge type, and when lifted at one end by means of large screws was carried on wheels and could be drawn back over the adjoining span.

It was a lengthy as well as a cumbersome operation, and when, in 1899, the ironwork portion of the viaduct had become too weak for the constantly increasing loads of developing traffic, it was completely renewed with a modern steel structure of four spans, one of which was a spring span, revolving on the centre pier and giving two clear openings. The piers carrying the girders are formed of columns 8ft. in diameter sunk through the sand down to solid rock, which was reached at a depth of about 90 feet below high water mark. The columns are steel cylinders filled with concrete, and were sunk into position by means of compressed air on the diving bell principle, and owing to the depth below water at high tide, the men excavating inside were finally working under a pressure of three atmospheres, or 45 lbs. to the square inch. The contractors were the Cleveland Bridge and Engineering Co. Ltd., of Darlington. In 1906, and the following two or three years, the timber portion of the viaduct was also completely renewed in the same material, the contractor in this case being Mr. Abraham Williams of Aberdovey, who had built, or helped to build, many of the old wooden bridges on the coast line. The total cost of the renewals was approximately £60,000, and it is no small achievement that they were carried out without a moment's stoppage in the traffic.

BARMOUTH BRIDGE
Reproduced from the "Great Western Magazine."

But even the original viaduct, old-fashioned as it may seem now, was a wonder in those days, and the fact that it carried (and still carries) a footpath as well as the railway, provides Barmouth with a promenade unrivalled in character and in range of panorama of river and mountains and sea anywhere in this country. For a time before it was completely finished a carriage was drawn over the bridge by horses, but in 1867 it was opened for regular traffic, and in the first train which crossed it into Barmouth rode the gentleman, who was under contract to make a meal of the locomotive. If he had forgotten his rash undertaking, he was very soon to receive a startling reminder. On safe arrival on the northern shore, the story goes, he was politely escorted by an official to a table laid for one, and was courteously requested to elect whether he would have the engine roast or boiled. Alas! for the frailty of human nature, more especially where a sense of humour might stand us in good stead. The sceptic, disillusioned, is stated to have failed to appreciate the joke!

Once the estuary was bridged, north of Barmouth, the constructional problems were simpler of solution, and when the contractors reached Minffordd, they were able to take advantage of an earlier engineering enterprise, no less remarkable than any railway building. In former days the sea had covered what is now called the Traeth, the broad valley of the Glaslyn, stretching from the hillocks of Penrhyndeudraeth to Moel-y-Gest, overlooking Portmadoc. The tides then surged several miles up this vale, and washed the walls of Llanfrothen churchyard, while vessels bore their freights almost up to Pont Aberglaslyn. In 1791 Mr. Madocks, following the example of earlier builders of sea walls in the district, purchased the Tan-yr-allt estate, and soon set to work to make dry land of a large part of the ocean bed. He erected what, in the locality, is commonly called a "cob," the great embankment which runs across the mouth of the former estuary, shut out the sea and recaptured 4,500 acres from its rapacious maw. Behind the shelter of this embankment (along the top of which the Festiniog Railway runs), the new line was comparatively easily carried over the marshy ground, and no greater gulf had to be bridged than the narrow channel in which the river, flowing down from the bosom of Snowdon, some eight or nine miles away, is now confined.

But there were other difficulties to be faced—difficulties not so easily overcome as even mountain torrents and sandy estuaries. The hand of the law was heavy upon the constructors, and even when the line was practically ready for opening, so long a delay took place in settling outstanding claims that the track became almost derelict. For these were anxious days for railway promoters. The rosy promise of rich revenues from remote Welsh lines failed to mature, and Mr. Savin, heavily weighted with the immensity of his undertakings, and crushed by the costly construction of his great hotels, sank under the burden. He faced his financial embarrassments with characteristic pluck, but it was a dark hour in the annals of British finance far beyond the boundaries of the Principality, amidst which came the sensational failure of the Overend and Gurney Bank, and, so far as the Welsh Coast Railway in particular was concerned, the interminable legal wrangles not only cost money, but postponed the hour at which the line could earn its keep.

Even under these adverse circumstances trains did occasionally run, carrying pigs from Pwllheli, or a small load of coal or timber for some outlying farmer or builder, or a passenger or two willing to take the risk of an adventurous journey liable at any moment to be brought to a sudden termination by the barriers of the bailiffs. But even bailiffs are human; and at night, when they slept, or were turned away by subtle hospitality at some neighbouring hostelry, journeys could be made, dashing down from Portmadoc to Barmouth and back with all the exhilaration of a secret expedition.

Eventually assistance came to the hard-pressed promoters, and the line was officially opened for traffic from Barmouth to Pwllheli on October 10th, 1867. But the number of trains often depended on the state of the exchequer, and sometimes quaint incidents would occur to break the monotony of events. One driver arriving from Pwllheli at Portmadoc, in the early days, discovering that there was no "staff" available to enable him to proceed to Penrhyndeudraeth according to regulations, was in considerable perplexity as to what to do, when an ingenious sub-official bethought him of a scheme, and fetching an old carpenter's auger, wrapped it round with paper, and thus armed by what perpetrated to be the badge of authority to go forward, the driver blew his whistle and off the train went on its hazardous way.

On another occasion an official of the line visiting one station master on this section was startled, in reply to his cheery inquiry as to whether all was well with him, to learn that "the only drawback was that he had the devil in his parlour." On his exclamation of incredulous alarm, the stationmaster said that he would show the official, if he would come and see. Entering the station house with some trepidation, he beheld in the middle of the parlour one of the iron fire-brackets, used to prevent water troughs from freezing in cold weather, popularly known among railway men as "devils." It seems that the builders had neglected to put in a grate, and the poor man had had to fall back on this diabolical method of keeping himself warm! The matter, no doubt, was quickly righted, for stationmasters, even then, were important functionaries, often wearing tall silk hats, though some of them were regarded as passing rich on 15/- or 16/- a week.

It was something, however, that, in the face of all these difficulties, financial and constructive, a line should be completed along this wandering coast at all. Only in one respect, indeed, did the original project fall short of attainment. The great objective of which the shareholders heard so much in earlier days—Porth Dinlleyn—was never reached. The line still terminates at Pwllheli, where, up to 1901, the station lay at arm's length from the town close to the harbour, which, in hot weather, used sometimes to alarm arriving visitors by its fishy odours. In 1901 power was obtained to carry the line into the centre of the town, where a new and commodious station now serves this popular health resort, the gateway to the mysterious fastnesses of Lleyn.

CHAPTER VIII. SOME EARLIER BRANCHES.

"Y ddel gerbydres welir—yn rhedeg
  Ar hyd ein dyffryn-dir,
 Ac yn gynt ar ei hynt hir
 Y fellten ni theithia filltir.

O ganol tre Llangynog—am naw
  Cychwyn wneir yn dalog,
 Fe'n ceir cyn tri'n fwy gwisgi na'r gog,
 A hoenus yn Llundain enwog." [91]

—A WELSH BARD.

The traveller along the main artery of the Cambrian, from Whitchurch to Aberystwyth, will note that, as he proceeds on his way, past the Welsh border foothills, and on by the waters of the Severn to the highlands of central Montgomeryshire, a series of more or less attractive lateral valleys branch off to the left, and still more definitely, to the right. Up some of these the eyes of ambitious engineers and railway promoters had often been cast as the main line was being constructed. No less eagerly did the residents at the remoter ends of these sequestered hollows among the hills look forward to the day when they might be linked up with the central system, and so brought into direct touch with the great world beyond.

There had, as we have seen, already been plans for carrying a line right up the Vyrnwy or the Tanat Valley, through the Berwyns to the vale of the Dee—the wonderful West Midland line which was to run from Shrewsbury to the shores of Cardigan Bay, over hill and down dale with "only one tunnel." But the route left Llanfyllin eight miles to the south, and Llanfyllin, as the largest town among these upland valleys, was not disposed to take that lying down. The Oswestry and Newtown line crossed the end of the vale, at Llanymynech, only nine miles away, and that was clearly the route by which the engineers could most easily construct a connective link. In the autumn of 1860, one of Llanfyllin's most prominent citizens, Mr. J. Pugh, had posted over to Oswestry, where he had an interview with Mr. Whalley. "Can you help us to get a railway?" Yes, anything in his power, the hon. Member for Peterboro' would do, and he was as good as his word. Within a month a crowded audience pressed into the Llanfyllin Town Hall to listen to the scheme which Mr. Whalley and his colleagues had to lay before them. The chair was taken by Mr. R. M. Bonner Maurice, of Bodynfoel, who had, it was happily recalled, presided at one of the meetings eight years earlier at Newtown out of which the germ of the

Montgomeryshire Railways sprang. This was, indeed, good augury, and when, not only Mr. Whalley and Mr. Johns, with their enthusiasm, but Mr. George Owen, with his plans in his pocket, came before them to show how the thing could be done, at a cost of some £60,000, enthusiasm rose high.

The meeting, however, was not "like Bridgnorth election, all on one side." Mr. A. C. Sheriff, of Worcester, manager of the West Midland Railway, existent, so far, merely on paper, was there too, only he had no plans in his pocket, and little more than vague notions in his head. "If" they did make a second tunnel, out of the Tanat Valley, then Llanfyllin should certainly be brought on to their main line, which would carry the farmers straight into Shrewsbury market. The farmers, however, did not want to go to Shrewsbury market. They wanted to go to Oswestry and Welshpool, and it was by Llanymynech that their way lay. So it scarcely needed Mr. Abraham Howell's warning to avoid the "shoals and pitfalls" which threatened any deviation from the branch line scheme. "Great companies," cried the redoubtable lawyer, "have been the bane of Montgomeryshire," and Llanfyllin shouted back that they would have none of them, whether they found they could tunnel out of the Tanat Valley or not. Besides, "if" the West Midland could not put Llanfyllin on the main line—and a very big "if" it seemed—then, Mr. Sheriff admitted, it would not touch the town at all.

So, sweeping aside all "ifs" and "buts," Llanfyllin voted for the Llanymynech branch. Whether it might be worked as an independent undertaking or as part of the Oswestry and Newtown Company's concern, mattered comparatively little. In either case, Mr. Savin was ready to guarantee a dividend of 4½ per cent., and Mr. Whalley had so much confidence in the firm of contractors that he would back the guarantee with his own name. Big companies should have no blighting and delaying influence on their little valley. Like the other local companies to which Mr. Howell alluded as examples of self-reliance, they would "trust to their own exertions," and since, as somebody said, the Oswestry and Newtown Railway was already a concrete fact, and no mere hypothetical proposition, it was agreed to "join heart and hand" with the company. A resolution to that effect was proposed by Mr. C. R. Jones, seconded by Mr. John Jones— two names long intimately associated in close comradeship with the public life of Llanfyllin—and carried unanimously; a similar conclusion being arrived at at a meeting of "a few of the most influential inhabitants of Llanymynech," with the Rev. J. Luxmoore, Rector, in the chair, later in the day.

Latest Cambrian Composite Bogey Coach, built for through traffic between Aberystwyth and Manchester.

As to the rival West Midland scheme, like the ogre in the fairy tale which ends happily ever afterwards, "little more was heard of it," at any rate as a great through route from Shrewsbury to the sea. The project was revived in the Parliamentary session of 1864, and a crowded meeting at Llanrhaiadr gave it tumultuous blessing in speech and bardic effusion. [94] But, though ultimately a line was constructed from Shrewsbury (as we have shown in a previous chapter) it got no further than the Nantmawr quarries, a few miles north-west of Llanymynech, and after running some years, became derelict, until revived under the Light Railways Act as the Shropshire and Montgomeryshire Railway. Not until 1904 did the Tanat Valley itself echo to the sound of any sort of railway coach, "lightning" or otherwise. Here again it was the Light Railways Act which made construction possible. The Tanat Valley Light Railway Company was formed, the directors being gentlemen interested in the locality, with Alderman Charles E. Williams, of Oswestry, as Chairman. After some controversy as to whether the line should be narrow guage, starting from Oswestry and running along the Morda Valley through Llansilin, or an ordinary guage extension of the mineral branch from Llynclys to Porthywaen, via Llanyblodwel, the latter plan was adopted, and, under pressure from the Earl of Bradford, a large local landowner, a connection was also formed over the old Nantmawr mineral line to Llanymynech. The railway which had its terminus at Llangynog has well served an important quarrying and agricultural district, but it has never flourished financially. For many years, indeed, the Company existed only in name, and in 1921 it was formally absorbed in the Cambrian, which had worked it, under agreement, from the outset.

But let us go back to the more successful enterprise in the neighbouring valley. The middle of July 1863 saw the Llanfyllin branch ready for traffic and on the seventeenth the opening ceremony took place. It included an excursion to Borth in twenty-three carriages packed with people, many of whom had never seen the sea. The train, we are told by a contemporary chronicler, failed to keep time, but who cared? There were some piquant scenes on the beach when the ladies, essaying to bathe, found themselves closely surrounded by "gentlemen" in anchored boats, but that, again, was a short-coming in the ordered programme which was readily overlooked! Anyhow, it seems, a good many people managed to miss the return train which "started punctually" at 1-30, arriving at Llanfyllin at half-past five, and so they also missed the dinner, presided over by the High Sheriff of Montgomeryshire, Mr. J. Dugdale, and the speeches, with which the official proceedings closed. The next day, following the precedent set at the opening of the Llanidloes and Newtown Railway, Messrs. Savin and Ward entertained the navvies to a "good substantial dinner" of their own, after which they, too, were entertained to a flow of oratory from the "big wigs" of the railway company and the locality, and another series of toasts were honoured with "three times three."

The promoters had cautiously qualified their promises as to the length of the branch by proposing to have its terminus at Llanfyllin for "the present." Some years later, when the Liverpool City Council, seeking fresh water supplies for their growing community, found a rich source in the valley of the Vyrnwy at Llanwddyn and constructed their giant works at what is now Lake Vyrnwy, thoughts began to turn to the prospect of a continuation of the railway in that direction, but it was not a practicable proposition. Up the Llanfyllin branch, however, there came the bulk of the stores, including the huge pipes, and the Portland cement for the bed of the lake. The cement was landed in bags at Aberdovey and from Llanfyllin a team of ninety-five horses was employed to draw it by road to the site of the works. Half were stabled at Llanfyllin and half at the Lake, and those in charge noted a curious fact. The horses living at the Lake went down empty in the morning and came back loaded in the afternoon, and in a few years were all out of condition, whereas those who started in the morning with their heavy load from Llanfyllin and returned empty later in the day were always in excellent fettle. To-day the development of the motor has solved many a transport problem where heavy loads are concerned, but Llanfyllin remains, perhaps, the most convenient approach to Lake Vyrnwy for the increasing number of visitors who go year by year to enjoy its scenic beauties and its piscatorial delights.

Less rapid success attended a similar enterprise a dozen miles away. While the good folks of Llanfyllin were pushing on with their branch, the residents of Llanfair Caereinion were asking themselves why they, too, should not have their railway. Here, also, the initial problem was one of route; but, instead of a somewhat easily disposed-of rivalry on the part of a competitive company, the crux here was the measure of support which could be won from the owner of the Powis estate, through which it would almost inevitably, in some form or another, have to pass. In July 1862 Mr.

R. D. Pryce of Cyfronaith, who was much interested in the development of the Llanfair district, asked the Earl of Powis to receive a deputation, but to a proposal that the line should go by the Black Pool dingle his lordship found himself unable to agree. The promoters were disappointed, for it seemed at the time, that no other way was feasible. But a month later another route was discovered, by way of Newton Lane, Berriew and Castle Caereinion and so by Melinyrhyd Gate to Llanfair; or, as an alternative suggestion, from Forden or Montgomery by the "Luggy Brook."

A meeting was held at Llanfair at which Mr. Edwin Hilton explained a scheme which was estimated to cost £60,000, of which £20,000 should first be raised in ordinary shares, the rest to be made up afterwards of preference shares and debentures. But nothing directly came of it, and it was not until October, 1864, that another proposal was formulated, this time of more ambitious character. This was a variation of the original Shrewsbury and West Midland route, which Llanfyllin had already laughed out of countenance, starting from Welshpool and making its way through Llanfair over (or rather under) the Berwyns to the Great Western system by the Dee. Mr. David Davies, on being consulted, favoured a 2ft. 3in. guage, though he advised that enough land should be taken and bridges built to accommodate an ordinary guage later if found necessary. The minimum speed on the narrow guage was to be fifteen miles an hour, and it was estimated that the average receipts would work out at £5 per mile.

Amongst the leading advocates of this scheme was Mr. Russel Aitken, a well-known civil engineer of Westminster, the home of many Welsh railway projects in those days. He got into correspondence with Lord Powis about it, pointing out that, as a beginning, the line might be made as far as Llanfair, and then the promoters might "wait and see." But Powis Castle was not so easily to be persuaded. The Earl considered a railway from Welshpool below Llanfair Road to Sylvaen Hall "very objectionable" and much preferred the alternative route of branching off the Llanfyllin line at Llansantffaid, via Pont Robert. This Mr. Aitken "could not successfully try to contest" and therefore "gave up the idea of trying for powers to construct the proposed railway," but he still thought a line "from Bala to Welshpool would pay and that it would be a great benefit to the country through which it passes." How far these prognostications may have been justified experience has never given us opportunity to ascertain. A railway through the mighty ramparts of the Berwyns is as remote an accomplishment to-day as it ever was; though, after many years, Llanfair itself was to obtain its narrow guage line, an inch less than Mr. Davies's original design, which, under the name of the Welshpool and Llanfair Light Railway, with the Earl's successor as its most enthusiastic promoter and chairman, was opened for traffic on April 4th, 1903, to be worked by the Cambrian as an important feeder to its main system.

The late CHIEF INSPECTOR GEORGE THOMAS, Of Oswestry, popularly known in his day as one of "The Three Georges," the other two, of course, being Mr. George Lewis, General Manager, and Mr. George Owen, Engineer.

The late GUARD CUDWORTH, Of Oswestry, for many a long year the highly esteemed custodian of the principal passenger trains on the Cambrian, beloved of all the travelling public.

A shorter branch, some five miles in length, from Abermule winding up the course of the Mule to the village of Kerry, was in course of construction while these other schemes were maturing or languishing. On Monday, March 2nd, 1863, the first engine puffed its way up the long incline (some of it as steep as 1 in 43) to Kerry, drawing one carriage, and on its arrival, after several stoppages on the way to "make steam," was met by a company of local ladies and gentlemen. It had been intended to indulge in some speechmaking, as befitted so auspicious an occasion, but the assembled guests were so absorbed in shaking hands with one another and looking at the engine, panting after its exertions, that the oratory was forgotten, and folks were content to offer their personal congratulations to Mr. Poundley, through whose enthusiasm and activities the branch was mainly built. It had also been arranged to attach to the train a truck of coal from Abermule to distribute amongst the poor, but this was more than the locomotive could accomplish. It went up the next day, and, no doubt, contributed to a wide endorsement of the views of the newspaper scribe, detailed to record these stirring events, that the branch was "everything Kerry can want."

Anyhow, with its still rare trains, it is all that Kerry has ever had, and possibly Kerry is still content.

The Kerry branch is also noteworthy for another thing, that it is the first arm of the system which diverges to the east of the main line. So does what was originally the first portion of the trunk, the line from Moat Lane to Llanidloes, later extended by the amalgamation with the Mid-Wales Railway, to Brecon, and so also does another diminutive line, another mile further, which, though not part of the Cambrian proper, deserves notice in these pages, if only for the personality of its former manager.

This is the Van line, which ran from Caersws (whose station is built on the site of an old Roman settlement) up to the Van mines, once productive enough of valuable lead ore, but now derelict. Constructed under the Railways Construction Facilities Act, 1864, the line was opened for mineral traffic on August 14th, 1871 and for passenger traffic on December 1st, 1873. It was leased to the Cambrian, but got into Chancery and was closed a few years later. While it ran many made pilgrimage along its short length, less for the purpose of traversing its rather uninteresting course than for a chance of conversing with one of the most notable characters, under whose charge the trains ran. To many Welshmen, indeed, who never travelled on or even heard, except perhaps quite incidentally, of the Van Railway, the name of John Ceiriog Hughes is a household word.

Born at Llanarmon-Dyffryn-Ceiriog, in Denbighshire, on September 25th, 1832, he passed his early years in the romantic vale of the Ceiriog, amidst the glowing memories of Huw Morris of Pont-y-Meibion. Beginning his business career in Manchester, he soon returned to his native land, and, after occupying a position as stationmaster at Llanidloes, was appointed to the management of this little line. The duties were not particularly arduous, and, in any case, "Ceiriog" was apt to take life with a light heart. Whether he sat in his office or in the cosy corner of some favourite rural inn the muse burned brightly within him, and, from his remote retreat among the hills which look down on the infant Severn, he poured out his soul in poetry, which ranks high in Celtic literature. Welsh verse always suffers in translation into the more cumbrous English, but there are many who have known the charm even of an Anglicised version of "Myvanwy Vychan," and when he died, in 1887, he was acclaimed by such an authority as the Rev. H. Elvet Lewis, to be "one of the best lyrical poets of Wales," who had "rendered excellent service to the national melodies of 'Cymru Fu' by writing words congenial to their spirit,—a work which Robert Burns did for Scottish melodies." He was buried in Llanwnog churchyard, where a simple plate marks his resting place, and friends and neighbours who attended the funeral service on the following Sunday did not feel that it was out of place that it should have been based on the text "Know ye not that there is . . . a great man fallen this day." They did know it, humble as his station might be; and more than one of his admirers has since visited the little deserted office where he worked on the Van line and ransacked its drawers and cupboards for hidden gems of poesy he might have left behind him. Alas! nothing more inspiring was ever found there than faded way-bills and torn invoices! But who shall say that there is no romance clinging close around even the humblest, and now the most woe-begone, of all the little offshoots of the Cambrian?

CHAPTER IX. CONSOLIDATION.

"Facility of communication begets 'community of interests,' which is the only treaty that is not a 'scrap of paper.'"—

THE LATE LORD FISHER.

Lord John Russell, it is said, used, in conversation with Queen Victoria, to date all political development from the Revolution of 1688. If those mystic figures signalize the birthday of Whiggery, in the political world, in much the same way we may date the constitution of the Cambrian, as we know it to-day, from the year 1864. In more than one way it was a notable period in Welsh railway annals. The various independent links in the chain were either completed and wholly or partially in working order, or in course of construction. Thanks to the influential efforts of the Earl of Powis, arrangements had been made with the Post Office and the London and North Western Railway Company, through Sir Richard Moon, for the conveyance of mails from Shrewsbury to Borth, the then terminus. Through working arrangements were also in force among the various local companies, and it was obvious that the time had come to face the problems of future policy. These were not altogether of simple solution.

A Group of Old Officials.

Standing—From left to right—The first figure is unidentified; Mr. Geo. Owen, Engineer; Mr. Henry Cattle, Traffic Manager. Seated—Mr. A. Walker, Locomotive Supt.; Mr. George Lewis, Secretary and General Manager; Mr. H. C. Corfield, Solicitor.

Very early in the year Mr. Abraham Howell was moved, in one of his frequent letters to the Earl of Powis, to warn his lordship that he scented "another crisis coming on in the affairs of the Welsh Railways." Once more there was division of opinion and "parties" were forming. Mr. Piercy and the majority of the directors were for extending "the" Welsh system so as to make it independent of the great companies and set aside existing agreements and obligations." Mr. Howell himself, with Mr. Savin and a minority on the Board, inclined rather to the course of accommodation with circumstances, making the best of the lines and properties of the companies as they stood, avoiding extensions and increasing capital, while cultivating friendly arrangements with neighbouring companies and so avoiding as much as possible Parliamentary and legal conflicts.

After all the tribulations through which these undertakings had passed the more politic and pacific course certainly had its advantages, but one Parliamentary adventure could not easily be avoided. Whether the policy was to be one of splendid isolation or of neighbourly friendship, the moment was obviously ripe for some measure of internal consolidation, and powers were sought for this purpose. The Bill had to pass through the now familiar ordeal of battle, both in the Committee of the House of Commons and in the House of Lords, when many of the old arguments and some new ones were skilfully marshalled on behalf of the Great Western Railway Company and rolled on the tongue of eminent and eloquent counsel. Even the little Bishop's Castle undertaking threw in its lot with the opposition, finding a powerful protagonist in Mr. Whalley. But the Cambrian had stout friends to put in the witness-box. Earl Vane proved a tough nut to crack in cross-examination. So did the Earl of Powis, still apparently tinged with a North Western bias. With the result that after much forensic oratory, closing appropriately on a reminder of "the troubles and difficulties the companies had gone through," and a well deserved "tribute to the energy and talent of their solicitor, Mr. Abraham Howell," the Amalgamation Bill, excluding for the time being the Welsh Coast line, was passed into law in July, 1864.

It set up a joint board, limited to a minimum of six and a maximum of twelve, the first directors chosen being those who had similarly served the several independent companies, some of whom, of course, had acted on more than one of these concerns. The following year, some previous difficulties being removed, the Welsh Coast Railway was brought into the combine, and the Cambrian then assumed the organic shape in which it remained until the further amalgamation with the Mid-Wales Railway in 1904.

Financially, however, the directors still swam in troubled waters. Creditors became impatient and began to press their claims. More than one suit was brought against the Company involving long and expensive proceedings in the Court of Chancery, and very early in 1868 it was found necessary to convene, at Oswestry, a meeting of the "mortgagees, holders of certificates of indebtedness and other creditors, and of the preference and ordinary proprietors for the consideration of the best means of dealing with the conflicting and other claims and interests of the company's creditors and proprietors and of passing such resolutions in regard thereto, or any of them, as might at such meeting be deemed expedient." To obtain some means of getting out of the financial morass in which the undertaking was floundering was "expedient" indeed, and it is hardly surprising to find that, in view of the many conflicts of interest, the assembly is recorded to have been both "large and influential." Mr. Bancroft presided in the absence of Earl Vane, chairman of the Company, and he was supported by the directors and officials who had done much to bring the Cambrian into existence and were now struggling to put it on its feet. The scheme which was laid before the meeting was long and complicated. More than one meeting was required to thrash matters out, but in the end a readjustment was arrived at, and a new scheme was adopted for constituting the board. From July 1st, 1868, until December 31st, 1878, it consisted of ten directors, four of whom were elected by the Coast Section and four by the Inland Section, the other two seats being in the nomination of Earl Vane and the Earl of Powis. The revenue from the whole undertakings went into a common fund, and, after deducting working expenses, the surplus was divided between the Coast and Inland Sections in certain proportions, to be determined by arbitrators and an umpire. Admirable as this arrangement might be in theory, in practice we know what generally happens when

> "United, yet divided, twain at once
> Sit two Kings of Brentford on one throne,"

and it is hardly astonishing that this form of dual authority should have led to a good deal of squabbling between the rival "monarchs." It proved, indeed, a cumbrous contrivance, and, when the period for its operation terminated, with the close of 1878, the constitution of the board was allowed to revert to the limits laid down under the Act of 1864, without any provision for sectional directors at all. During these intervening years, indeed, questions of finance and of the upkeep of the lines were still for ever cropping up, and not always as readily disposed of. It is a long and dreary story of the inevitable struggles with ways and means which so often marks the life of pioneer undertakings. For years these Chancery suits hung like chains about the company's neck, and even into the eighties the directors were never free from sudden embarrassments and never knew from what quarter they might proceed.

One such difficulty, indeed, ultimately proved a blessing in disguise. In 1884, at the instance of the Company's bankers, the line was placed in the hands of a Receiver, Mr. John Conacher, fortunately, being chosen for this office. The line was ripe for a great and final effort to place the undertaking on a firmer footing, and, together with the late Mr. A. C. Humphreys-Owen, Mr. Conacher drew up a scheme of arrangement between the Company and its creditors under which about seventy different stocks were consolidated into ten; and it was their patient and skilful work in thus formulating what became known as the scheme of 1885, that laid the foundation of the Company's improved financial position of which the proprietors and the public have reaped the benefit in subsequent years.

Meantime, however, other matters not directly bearing on finance, engaged the attention of the directors. Amongst these was the question of the works, which it was found necessary to erect, since the Company was working its own line. In July 1864, the inhabitants of Welshpool, conscious of the prominent part which the town had played in the inauguration of the Oswestry and Newtown Railway, presented a memorial to the board in which they urged its central position on the system and the recent completion of the waterworks as strong arguments for favourable consideration of the borough's claims to such an advantage. Nor was it without an eye to future development that Welshpool station was built in a manner capable of allowing its upper stories to be used as the Company's offices. Here, for the brief space, the offices were, but in both these cases ambitious Poolonians were doomed to disappointment.

The late MR. A. C. HUMPHREYS-OWEN, M.P.
Chairman, 1890-1905.

The official headquarters of the Newtown and Machynlleth Railway Company were destined for some time to remain at Machynlleth, where Mr. David Howell, its secretary, practised as a solicitor; but in January 1862 the staff of the Oswestry and Newtown had removed from Welshpool, and, together with those of the Llanidloes and Newtown, the Oswestry, Ellesmere and Whitchurch, the Buckley and the Wrexham Mold and Connah's Quay, jointly occupied two rooms on the second floor of No. 9a, Cannon Row, Westminster, Mr. George Lewis being secretary of all five companies. On the floor below the Aberystwyth and Welsh Coast Company cohabited with some dozen slate and stone companies, while Mr. Benjamin Piercy sat in state hard by in Great George Street, and Mr. Thomas Savin weaved his ambitious schemes around the corner, at No. 7, Delahay Street, with Mr. James Fraser (father of the auditor of the Cambrian in recent years) acting, under power of attorney, as his manager. This proved quite a convenient arrangement so long as Parliamentary Committee work absorbed much of the time of these officials, and here all the companies held their board meetings, generally on the same day.

There were stirring times without, and it is scarcely strange if Cannon Row did not live up to the reputation of its suggestive name. Rows, indeed, were frequent and occasionally threatened to reverberate beyond the walls of the official sanctum. There is an old and honoured Cambrian official, then a young clerk sitting at his desk in the office above the board room, who remembers the occasion when an extraordinary scene was enacted on that dusty little stage. From a scuffle of some sort in the board room Mr. Gartside, a Director of the Oswestry and Newtown Railway Company, beat a hasty retreat up the stairs to the clerk's room, closely pursued by Mr. Whalley. Mr. Gartside being rather portly, was much out of breath, and suddenly pausing and turning round to recover himself on gaining the hearthrug he received Mr. Whalley's fist full in the stomach, which completed his exhaustion. Recovering his breath and as much of his dignity as the circumstances would permit, the disabled Director appealing dramatically to the astonished clerks, exclaimed "Gentlemen, I call on you to witness that the hon. Member for Peterboro' has struck me." But the clerks unable to grapple with so unaccustomed a situation, beat a hasty retreat, and nothing more was heard of what was presumably a more or less accidental "assault."

From Great George Street, the offices were subsequently moved to No. 3, Westminster Chambers, and soon after Mr. Savin's failure, in 1866, when the directors took over the working of the line from the unfortunate lessee, after a short trial of another London office, the Secretary and his staff, in August of that year, packed up pens, ink, paper and documents and settled themselves in Oswestry, where they have since remained. In Oswestry, too, on a site under the Shelf Bank, close to where the first sod on the Ellesmere and Oswestry line was cut, the works were erected and have continued to be maintained.

OSWESTRY STATION AND COMPANY'S HEAD OFFICES
Reproduced from the "Great Western Magazine"

On a subsequent occasion, however, they were the ostensible cause of one of those sudden storms which, as we have said, from time to time assailed the board-room or even periodical assemblies of the proprietors. On this occasion it was, indeed, a bolt from the blue. A few days before the date fixed for the half yearly meeting, at Crewe, in February 1879, there had been placed in the hands of the shareholders a pamphlet bearing the innocent title "Cambrian Railways Workshops." But, when they read it, the recipients discovered that, whatever the reason for the choice of such a heading, the sermon was founded on a much wider text. It traversed the whole policy of the Board, the constitution of the Company and the management of its property, and it was written in highly censorious terms. That, in itself, might have been of comparatively little moment, for the directors were not without their critics—no directors of public companies ever are. But the author, who did not withhold his name, was Mr. David Davies, constructor of much of the line and now one of the most influential directors. Here, apparently, was a matter for serious concern, and the seriousness was not diminished when to the pamphlet itself was added a speech, at the shareholders' meeting, in which Mr. Davies did not scruple to suggest that the line was being expensively worked, that the rolling stock had not been adequately maintained, that the road was defective and that, some of the stock being worthless, the whole undertaking was in a false position. It was what Earl Vane (now become Marquess of Londonderry), who presided, called "a stab in the dark." The stab in the open with which Mr. Davies followed it up was certainly not less sensational. He declared that "the line at the moment was not safe, and he should not be at all surprised to see the rails sprinkled with human blood before they were very much older." He alleged that a fellow director (Mr.

S. H. Hadley) had expressed a wish to see the Oswestry shops burnt down and new shops erected at Aberystwyth instead. The balance-sheet was "an insult." He washed his hands of the whole affair and demanded a Committee of Inquiry. A hub-bub ensued, amidst which it was not impertinently pointed out that Mr. Davies had himself laid much of the road which he now condemned, and, backed by a letter from Mr. George Owen, the engineer, it was shown that his strictures on its existing condition were unsubstantiated by facts. But Mr. Davies stuck to his guns, and before what was well described in the local Press as "a stormy meeting" terminated, he had left the room and his seat on the Board. It was a matter of doubt, for some moments, whether the noble Chairman would not go too, but, happily, he discovered enough signs of confidence among the proprietors present to encourage him to continue his thankless task.

It was a tremendous tempest while it lasted, but it was soon over. At the next half-yearly meeting, in the following August, the directors were able to report that, instead of spilt blood, the summer had brought a considerably increased weight of tourist traffic, hearty congratulations were showered on Mr. George Lewis, the Secretary, on his efficient administration of the line, and Capt. R. D. Pryce, presiding, in the absence of the Marquess, concluded the proceedings on a happy note of assurance that directors and shareholders were "of one mind," and full of sanguine expectations as to the future of their undertaking. The throes of consolidation are sometimes not less severe than those of birth itself, but they can be as successfully survived.

CHAPTER X. INCIDENTS AND ACCIDENTS.

> "Railway travelling is safer than walking, riding, driving, than going up and down stairs . . . and even safer than eating, because it is a fact that more people choke themselves in England than are killed on all the railways of the United Kingdom."—THE LATE SIR EDWARD WATKIN.

Looking back on considerably more than half a century of history it is no small tribute to human care and human ingenuity that serious accidents on the Cambrian Railways have been relatively rare. This is all the more remarkable because all but some twelve miles of its total length, and up to a few years ago, not even as much as that, has had to be worked on a single line, and with the rapidly increasing tourist traffic of recent times, this has placed a strain on both the human and the metallic machine which may easily try the strongest nerves and the most powerful appliances. Obviously it is due to the special care taken in management, and observed, with few if tragic exceptions, by those directly responsible for the working of the trains.

Early in their inception, elaborate regulations were drawn up by the organisers of the original local undertakings, of which a copy, issued by the Oswestry and Newtown Company, as adopted "at a meeting of the Board of Directors, held on Saturday, the 25th February, 1860," and preserved among the papers of the late Mr. David Howell of Machynlleth, gives some interesting indication. It is bound in vellum, fitted with a clasp, and adorned within with a series of woodcuts, descriptive of the old-day signalman, clad in tall hat, tail coat and white trousers, explanatory of the hand signal code, with flags, which preceded the more general use of the modern signals, controlled from a signal box. Following the precept, made familiar by the nursery rhymes of our childhood, it informs us that

> "RED is a signal of DANGER, and to STOP.
>
> GREEN is a signal of CAUTION, and to GO SLOWLY.
>
> WHITE is a Signal of ALL RIGHT, and to GO ON.

As an additional precaution, should no flag be handy, it warns drivers that "anything moved violently up and down or a man holding both hands up is a sign of danger."

Some of these early regulations were extremely primitive. For instance, long before the scientific system of the block telegraph and the tablet were thought out, it was deemed sufficient to ordain that "On a Train or Engine stopping at or passing an intermediate station or Junction, a STOP Signal must be exhibited for FIVE minutes, after which a CAUTION Signal must be exhibited for FIVE minutes more." After that, apparently, any train might proceed—and take its risk of the one in front having reached the next signalling point! At level crossings at any distance from the signalman, the gate-keeper was advised to "ring a small hand-bell, or use a whistle to call the attention of the signalman, who must then put up his 'Danger' signals."

An Early Cambrian Passenger Engine (Original Form).

An Ex-M&M.

The guard of the first passenger train from Oswestry was instructed to "set his timepiece by the Platform Clock, and give the Clerk at every station the time, so that he may regulate the clock at his station by it," and similar arrangements operated up the branch lines. Porters were told that on the arrival of a train they were to "walk the length of the platform and call out, in a clear and audible voice, the name of the station opposite the window of each carriage; and at Junctions the doors of every carriage must be opened, and the various changes announced to all passengers"—a regulation which, if still on the rule-book, is, like that against receiving tips, nowadays more often honoured in the breach than in the observance. It was even felt obligatory to include a regulation as to what should be done if a train should arrive before its advertised time, though it must appear a little superfluous to those who remember the ways of the Cambrian in those happy days, when a captious correspondent could write to the local Press to aver that, after seeing his father off at Welshpool station, he was able to ride on horseback to Oswestry and meet him on his arrival there! It was certainly a remarkable feat—though, perhaps, not so remarkable either—for, as "an official" of the Company was moved to explain in a subsequent issue, the old gentleman must have travelled by a goods train, to which passenger coaches were attached "for the convenience of the public," and it "often did not leave Welshpool until an hour after the advertised time."

Those "mixed trains" survived until some thirty years ago, when an unregenerate Board of Trade regulation prohibited them, and the wonderful jolts and jars which the public experienced for their "convenience" and the benefit of their liver, if not their nerves, became a thing of the past. But, as an old driver remarked to the writer not long ago,—"It was very comfortable working in those days," and no doubt, for the traffic staff, it was.

We may smile to-day at some of these old ordinances and habits, but traffic then was not as congested as it is on an August day now, when thousands of tourists are being carried in heavily ladened trains to the coast of Cardigan Bay. The rolling stock at that time was as light as the signals were haphazard. We have read of references, in these early days, to "powerful" engines; but they were mere pigmies to the modern locomotive, and some of those pioneer machines which were the pride of the dale sixty years ago have been relegated long since to the humble duty of the shunting yard, or rebuilt altogether.

An Early Cambrian Tank Engine
(Original Form).

As Re-built.

An old engineman, writing some little time since in the "Cambrian News," gives an interesting retrospect of the "comforts" of railway travel on the Cambrian in those early days. "The original passenger rolling stock on service on the line when opened," he says, "was of a small four-wheeled type, similar in construction to the coaches on other company's lines; about 25 feet long over all, 13 feet wheel base, or half the length and a third the weight of the bogie stock of the present day. The coaches were built by contract, the work being divided between two well-known firms of builders,—the Ashbury Co., Manchester, and the Metropolitan Railway Carriage and Wagon Company, Birmingham. The Ashbury stock was slightly larger with more head room than the Metropolitan. The coaches were built of the very best material, the lower part of body being painted a dark brown, the upper part, from the door handles to roof, a cream colour. [114] Each coach weighed about 8 tons. The 'third class' coaches were made up of five compartments or semi-compartments. Cross seats, back to back sittings for five aside—accommodation for fifty passengers—bare boards for the seats, straight up backs, open from end to end. Our forefathers evidently believed, when constructing rolling stock, in fresh air in abundance instead of the closed up compartment of late years. The thirds were lighted at dusk with two glass globe oil lamps fixed in the roof, one at each end of the coach. Firsts and seconds were provided with a lamp for each compartment. The only other difference between the seconds and thirds was that the seats of the seconds were partly covered with black oilcloth. The latter carriage proved unremunerative, the public hardly ever patronising seconds. Therefore they were abolished. In addition to the ordinary screw coupling, coaches in those days were provided with side chains as security in case of breaking loose on the journey. Side chains, however, were abolished on the advent of the continuous brake. The buffers were provided with wooden block facings with a view of silencing and to prevent friction when travelling round curves—not at all a bad idea either. Wheels in those days were constructed entirely of iron with straight axles and spokes, not wooden blocked as at present to deaden noise. Owing to the lightness of the stock, when travelling at a fair rate of speed, oscillation occurred and passengers had to sit firm and fast, which everyone in those days seemed to enjoy."

Anyhow, there was plenty of fun to be got out of the experience. "The doors of the old coaches were narrow, and many a tussle to get inside occurred. One lady in particular who was very stout and a regular passenger on a certain train, always had to be assisted both in and out—the stationmaster pulling and the guard pushing, while the fireman was enjoying the joke. One morning, when the train was a few minutes late, the guard came running up to the front with his 'Hurry up, Missis,' when the old dame, with her two baskets, an umbrella, similar in size to a modern camping tent, and a crinoline fashionable in mid-Victorian days, got firmly wedged in the door way, whereupon some wag suggested that, to expedite departure, a break-down gang and crane should be sent for and the lady hoisted into an open cattle waggon."

II.

But even with all the care which the management enjoined from the first, accidents were, perhaps, not altogether unavoidable. Sometimes the errant "human factor" showed itself in tragic fashion even in those distant days. By a melancholy coincidence, the first serious mishap occurred close to Abermule, a name since associated in the public memory with the last and the worst catastrophe in Cambrian annals.

It was on a November morning in 1861 that a goods train leaving Newtown for Welshpool, called at Abermule, where they picked up three wagons and some water. But, unfortunately, there was time—or they thought there was time—for the driver, fireman, and guard to adjourn to the adjacent inn, where they took up something rather stronger than the engine's refreshment. Time fled, as it is apt to do in such circumstances, and when the staff rejoined the train, an effort appears to have been made to gain lost minutes, with the result that the train ran off the line, and driver, known to his comrades as "Hell-fire Jack," and fireman were killed. An inquest was held before Dr. Slyman, coroner, one of the most enthusiastic promoters of the Montgomeryshire lines, and the jury solemnly found that "the accident was the result of furious driving," but they exonerated from blame everyone but "the unfortunate driver."

An Early Cambrian Coach with its Makers.

But the "human factor" is not the only element of nature with which railway management has to contend. Another, not less serious in its potential consequences, was brought to mind in sinister fashion a few years later, when, during the winter storms of 1868, the Severn and its tributaries rose in flood with such alarming rapidity that the driver of an early morning goods train from Machynlleth to Newtown found, as he ran down the long decline from Talerddig past Carno, that the water was washing over the footplate of the engine, and nearly put out the fire. He naturally bethought him of the wooden bridge over the Severn at Caersws, but, after, careful examination, it was safely crossed. On the return journey, however, the bridge was being carefully approached once more, when, in the dim dawn of a February morning, the engine suddenly toppled-over the embankment abutting on the structure. The floods had washed away the earthworks, though the beams of the bridge itself held fast, and driver and fireman were killed. Word was sent to Oswestry and Aberystwyth, and in the first passenger train from the latter place Capt. Pryce, one of the directors, and Mr. Elias, the traffic manager, were travelling to the scene of the disaster, when it was discovered that another bridge, near Pontdolgoch, was giving way under pressure of the torrent, and the train, crowded with passengers, was only held up just in time to avert what could not have failed to prove a catastrophe far more tragic in extent.

Wild rumours quickly spread concerning the cause and nature of the actual mishap, it being freely stated by sensation-mongers that the Severn bridge had collapsed; but Mr. David Davies, who had been its builder and was now a director of the Company, was able to show that, despite the exceptional strain on the construction, the bridge had resisted the force of the flood and was as firm as ever. Wooden bridges, however, have now had their day, and in recent years have, in all important cases, under the enterprising supervision of Mr. G. C. McDonald, the Company's engineer and locomotive superintendent, been replaced with iron girders, to the undisguised regret of some old-fashioned believers in the efficacy of British oak!

This section of the line, indeed, flanked not only by the rivers liable to flood, but curving its way up steep gradients, over high embankments and through deep cuttings, is necessarily more subject to mishaps than a level road, and it is hardly astonishing that it has been the scene of more than one awkward circumstance. Among them is the story, still told more or less sotto voce, of how, close to this spot, the driver of an express goods train, long ago, might have killed the then Chairman of the Company! The night was wet, and the driver, accustomed to a straight run down the bank to Moat Lane, was astonished to find the signals against him at Carno. He applied the brakes, but it was no easy matter suddenly to curb the speed of a heavy train, and he floundered on, right into a "special" toiling up the hill bearing Earl Vane home to Machynlleth. [118] Happily for everyone concerned, no great damage was done; Board of Trade officials were less inquisitive in those days, and it seems to have been easier then than it is now to "keep things out of the newspapers"!

Less easy to hide was the huge landslide, many years later, of a portion of Talerddig cutting, though on this occasion no accident resulted to any train, and the worst fate that befel the passengers was that, during the considerable time occupied in clearing the line—it was at the height of the tourist season, too—they and their baggage had to be conveyed by road for a mile or two, an arduous task accomplished by the Company's officials without a single mishap.

Such happenings in such a character of country are practically inevitable, but it was not until the Cambrian had been in existence, as a combined organisation, for nearly twenty years, that its story was interrupted, through such a cause, by what was truly described as "the most alarming accident which had ever occurred on the system." In point of death-roll it was not more melancholy than that at Caersws, but its scene and its dramatic nature provided a new feature which intimately touched the public imagination. For it was the first serious disaster in the annals of these undertakings to a passenger train, and, though not one of them was even injured, the hairbreadth escape of several was thrilling enough.

On New Year's Day, 1883, the evening train from Machynlleth for the coast line, drawn by the "Pegasus," driven by William Davies, whose fireman bore a similar name, on reaching the Barmouth end of the Friog decline, built on the shelf of the rock overlooking the sea, struck a mass of several tons of soil, which had suddenly fallen from the steep embankment, together with a portion of retaining wall. The engine and tender appear to have passed the obstruction and then were hurled to the rocks below. Most fortunately the couplings between the tender and the coaches broke, and though the first carriage overturned, and lay perilously poised over the ledge, it did not fall. The next coach also overturned, but in safer position, and probably held up the first.

The remaining coach, which contained most of the passengers, and the van remained on the rails. Amongst those in the train was Captain Pryce, once more fortunate in his deliverance from death, and he and others immediately did what was possible to release the rest from danger. In the overhanging carriage was one old lady, Mrs. Lloyd, of Welshpool, a well-known character at Towyn, where she carried on a successful business in merchandise, and, save for severe and very natural fright, she was got out without sustaining further harm.

The news of the accident soon spread abroad, and reached Dolgelley, where a great Eisteddfod was being held. From this assembly Dr. Hugh Jones and Dr. Edward Jones, well-known medical men over the countryside, with others, hurried to the scene. But the driver and fireman were beyond the range of their skill. With bashed heads they lay, the former in the tender and latter beside the "Pegasus," on the huge rocks that flank the shore. Searching inquiry was made into the cause of the accident, and though evidence was forthcoming that the utmost care was taken to watch that section of the line, and Mr. George Owen, the engineer, and Mr. Liller, the traffic manager, were able to show that all the recommendations and regulations of the Board of Trade officials had been complied with in protecting this awkward cutting, the jury considered the place unsafe and hoped the Railway Company would "do something to prevent occurrence of a similar accident."

Such occurrences, alas! are not entirely within the compass of human power to control, but, as a matter of fact, no such "similar accident" has during its history ever happened at Friog or anywhere else on the Cambrian system. It was, indeed, not for more than fourteen years that serious catastrophe attended the working of the railway, and then the cause seems to have been as uncontrollable as ever. Late one Friday evening in June, 1897, a Sunday School excursion train from Royton in Lancashire, drawn by two engines, was returning from Barmouth, and, close to Welshampton station, only a few miles short of quitting the Cambrian at Whitchurch, left the rails, overturning several coaches and telescoping others. The circumstances were the more pathetic by reason of the fact that most of the passengers were children, homeward bound, after a joyous day by the sea. Nine were killed outright, two died later in hospital, and many others were more or less seriously injured. Dr. R. de la Poer Beresford of Oswestry, medical officer to the Cambrian Railway Co., and many other professional and lay helpers, rendered gallant service, and the railway ambulance corps were a valuable adjunct in the arduous task of dealing with the great work of tending the wounded. There was some little difficulty in ascertaining the exact cause of the accident, but the Coroner's jury were satisfied that there was "no negligence on the part of any of the officials," and were of opinion that the disaster would not have happened but for a Lancashire and Yorkshire four-wheeled brake van in the front of the train, which, it was stated, had been "running rough." Searchers after portents were quick to recal that in his famous "Almanack," exactly opposite the actual date of the disaster, "Old Moore" had stated that he was "afraid he must foretell a terrible railway collision in the middle of June." It was not a collision, but the gift of prophecy received sufficient endorsement to create no small sensation amongst country folk. Nor is this part of our story, unfortunately, complete without reference to an actual head-on collision,—an occurrence extremely rare in British railway annals—of even more appalling result in loss of life, than Welshampton. Of that day, early in 1921 when, through a most extraordinary and tragic series of misunderstandings amongst the staff at Abermule station the slow down train was allowed to proceed towards Newtown to meet the up express from Aberystwyth, on the curve a mile away, such vivid memories still linger that little need be recounted here of its harrowing details. The total death-roll, the largest in Cambrian records, was 17, and the victims included one of the most esteemed of the directorate, Lord Herbert Vane-Tempest. Here, at any rate, it was again that mysterious element, "the human factor," rather than any condition of the works or of the rolling stock used which played its melancholy part, and of that it is sufficient to say that the most interesting feature of the protracted official inquiry into the circumstances was the fact that the men concerned were represented at the inquest by the Rt. Hon. J. H. Thomas, M.P., as General Secretary of the National Union of Railwaymen, and his skilful conduct of the case was, apparently, a notable and important influence in determining the final—and reconsidered—verdict of the coroners jury.

The late LORD HERBERT VANE-TEMPEST,
a Director of the Company, who was fatally
injured in the Abermule accident, 1921.

III.

But these are sorrowful records from which we gladly turn to the lighter side of railway annals. As a link between them we may mention one "accident" which happily unattended with very serious results in itself, was the direct cause of a famous, and at the time, a sensational "incident." In 1887 the down morning mail train ran off the line at Ellesmere and it was held that this was due to delay on the part of the porter in not being at the points in time to work them properly. For at this time the interlocking system, made compulsory under the Act of 1889, had not been installed, and the safety of trains depended on due attention to the pointsman's functions. When, in 1891, a Committee of the House of Commons, of which Sir Michael Hicks-Beach was chairman, sat to inquire into the length of railway hours, the Ellesmere mishap was brought up as an example of what occurred when railway servants were expected to work for long stretches, though Mr. John Conacher (who had joined the Company's staff in 1865, become secretary on the retirement of Mr. George Lewis in 1882, and later had succeeded to the managership) was able to produce evidence that it was not so much weariness of the flesh as the fact that the porter was playing cards with a postman waiting with the mails and a stranded passenger waiting for the train which led to his late arrival at the points.

The porter was consequently dismissed, whereupon a memorial praying for his re-instatement was signed, amongst others, by the then Ellesmere stationmaster, the late Mr. John Hood. This appeared to the management so undesirable an attitude for a stationmaster to take in the matter of service discipline that he was temporarily suspended and removed from Ellesmere,—a step which, it was publicly explained, had been contemplated some years before the accident, but not carried out,—to Montgomery. Mr. Hood himself gave evidence before the Parliamentary Committee, alleging that the mishap was due to the rotten condition of the permanent way, and though this created a good deal of sensation and alarm, public assurance was promptly restored when it was pointed out that such a conclusion was entirely rebutted by the report issued by the Board of Trade Inspector as a result of his personal examination of the line immediately after the accident.

Probably little, if anything, more might have been heard of the affair, for the Select Committee had risen for the Parliamentary recess, were it not that the directors, carrying out a detailed examination of their own into the circumstances brought to light again by the inquiry, had laid before them a recommendation by their chief officials on which, rightly or wrongly, wisely or unwisely, they decided to dispense with Mr. Hood's services altogether. Mr. Hood was summoned to Crewe, where he had an interview with the Chairman of the Company, Mr. J. F. Buckley, who was accompanied by two of his colleagues on the Board,—Mr. Bailey-Hawkins and Mr. J. W. Maclure, M.P., and Mr. Conacher, the manager, but to a memorial in favour of the stationmaster's reinstatement, they declined to accede.

The fat was now in the fire, and a very fierce blaze ensued. It lit up the industrial world, then struggling into organic solidarity, with lurid flames, and there were those who had some trading or personal grievance against the company, who not less eagerly threw on fresh fuel of their own. Protest meetings were held at Wrexham and Newtown, at which resolutions were carried condemnatory of "excessive hours," and the late Mr. A. C. Humphreys-Owen, of Glansevern, though he had not been present at the Crewe conclave, was, as a director of the Company and a prospective Parliamentary candidate for the Denbigh Boroughs, singled out for special attack, and as warmly defended by some of his friends.

Mr. Harford, general secretary of the Amalgamated Society of Railway Servants of the United Kingdom, with what was, perhaps, an unconscious gift of prophecy, declared that "little railways were a gigantic mistake, and the sooner the better they are taken over by some larger concern, for the workmen and the shareholders." The Labour Press echoed with resounding phrases about "Cambrian tyranny," and "victimisation," and Mr. Hood was acclaimed a martyr of overbearing officialism.

More serious was the attitude and the action of Parliament. The House of Commons, ever quick to resent any appearance of tampering with its "privileges," were sensitive to the suggestion of what seemed to them some interference with a witness before their Select Committee, and not long after the new Session opened, in 1892, Mr. Conacher, who had, meanwhile, left the Cambrian, to the regret of the Board and many others, to assume the larger responsibility of management of the North British Railway Co., was summoned from Edinburgh to appear, with Mr. Buckley and Mr. Bailey-Hawkins, at the Bar of the House to receive the admonition of Mr. Speaker Peel. Mr. (afterwards Sir John) Maclure, being a Member of the House, was at the same time required to stand in his place, where, with bowed head, that burly and genial gentleman, looked very like a schoolboy listening to the stern rebuke of a formidable headmaster!

"Toby M.P.," glancing down from his seat in the Press Gallery on this rare and impressive scene, has described it in the pages of "Punch" in characteristic fashion:—

> "Thursday, April 7th.
>
> "The Chairman of Cambrian Railways held a special meeting at Bar. It was attended by Mr. Bailey-Hawkins, and Mr. John Conacher, Manager of the Company . . . The latter, resolved to sell his life dearly, brought in his umbrella, which gave him a quite casual hope-I-don't-intrude appearance as he stood at the Bar. Members, at first disposed to regard the whole matter as a joke, cheered Maclure when he came in at a half-trot; laughed when the Bar pulled out, difficulty arose about making both ends meet . . . Bursts of laughter and buzz of conversation in all parts of the House; general aspect more like appearance at theatre on Boxing Night, when audience waits for curtain to rise on new pantomime. Only the Speaker grave, even solemn; his voice occasionally rising above the merry din with stern cry of 'Order! Order!'
>
> "Hicks-Beach's speech gave new and more serious turn to affairs. Concluded with Motion declaring Directors guilty of Breach of Privilege and sentencing them to admonition. But speech itself clearly made out that Directors were blameless; all the bother lying at door of Railway Servant who had been dismissed. Speech, in short, turned its back on Resolution. This riled the Radicals; not to be soothed even by Mr. G. interposing in favourite character as Grand Old Pacificator. Storm raged

all night; division after division taken; finally, long past midnight, Directors again brought up to the Bar, the worn, almost shrivelled, appearance of Conacher's umbrella testifying to the mental suffering undergone during the seven hours that had passed since last they stood there.

"Speaker, with awful mien and in terrible tones, 'admonished' them; and so to bed."

The chief actors in this arresting and peculiar drama have now all past from the stage, almost the last survivor, Mr. Hood himself, dying in 1920, after a long career of public service in the local administration of civic affairs at Ellesmere, and not before, through the gracious good offices of the last General Manager, Mr. Samuel Williamson, full and formal reconciliation had taken place between him and the Company.

Four General Managers.

Rare, indeed, is such an "incident" in the annals of any British Railway. Much rarer, at any rate, than another cause for special managerial anxiety, though not untinged with pride,—the conveyance of a Royal passenger. In this respect the Company, particularly in more recent years, has borne its full share of responsibility and sustained it with adequate cause for self satisfaction. Queen Victoria, though she visited North Wales in the eighties, travelled by another route, and the first Royal train to pass over any part of the Cambrian system was that which bore King Edward VII.

and Queen Alexandra, when Prince and Princess of Wales, on their visit to Machynlleth and Aberystwyth, for the former's installation as Chancellor of the University of Wales in the middle of June, 1896, and on the same occasion another distinguished traveller along the line from Wrexham to Aberystwyth was Mr. Gladstone.

Eight years later, in July 1904, the late King and his Consort journeyed over the Mid-Wales section to Rhayader, to participate in the opening of the Birmingham Water Works, and thence to Welshpool on their way to London. On March 16th, 1910, King George, as Prince of Wales, passed over the Cambrian on his way to Four Crosses, to perform a similar ceremony in connection with the extension of the Liverpool Waterworks at Lake Vyrnwy, and the longest of all monarchical tours over the system was when, in the middle of July, 1911, King George, Queen Mary, and other members of the Royal family proceeded from Carnarvon via Afonwen and the Coast section to Machynlleth as guests at Plâs Machynlleth, the following day to Aberystwyth for the foundation stone-laying of the Welsh National Library, and two days later, from Machynlleth to Whitchurch on their way to Scotland.

The last Royal journey was a short one, again over the Mid-Wales section, in July 1920, to enable the King to inaugurate the Welsh National Memorial institution at Talgarth, on which occasion his Majesty was graciously pleased to express high appreciation of the facilities ever afforded by the Board and management whenever he travelled over their system. And on this gratifying note we may appropriately bring our record of Cambrian "incidents" to a close.

CHAPTER XI. THE CAMBRIAN OF TO-DAY.

"To stretch the octave 'twixt the dream and deed,
Ah! that's the thrill."—RICHARD LE GALLIENNE.

I.

And so, by devious routes and with many a halt by the way, we come to the Cambrian of to-day. In such a chronicle as this demarcations of time must necessarily appear more or less arbitrary, and if we include under this heading a period which goes back to 1904, it is merely because it is from that year the system has, with only some subsequent minor extensions in mileage, assumed the organic form familiar to us at the present time. For it was then that the policy of amalgamation, entered upon forty years earlier with the consolidation of the various independent companies, was carried forward another important stage, and it is since that date the most significant developments, both in road and rolling stock, made necessary by the ever-increasing demands of modern traffic conditions, have mainly been accomplished.

Officers of the Cambrian Railways at the date of Amalgamation,
March 25th, 1922.

As far back as February 1888, the question of merging the Mid-Wales Railway came before the Cambrian directors, under the earnest pressure of Mr. Benjamin Piercy. It was not long before even wider schemes of mutual co-operation among the railways of the Principality were being publicly discussed, under the aegis of what was termed the Welsh Railway Union, for which facilities were sought, by means of a private Bill. A deputation, introduced by Sir George Osborne Morgan (as he afterwards became) and headed by Mr. (later Sir John) Maclure and Sir Theodore Martin, waited on

Sir Michael-Hicks Beach, at the Board of Trade. Under this scheme all the lesser Welsh railways were to form a link for through traffic, by way of the projected Dee Bridge and Wrexham to South Wales; but, though nothing materialised at the time, there was something of intelligent anticipation about the appointment, in 1891, of Mr. Conacher, as manager of the Neath and Brecon Railway, one of the parties to the proposal, in addition to his management of the Cambrian. Very soon afterwards, however, Mr. Conacher left for the North British and the joint office was terminated. But another significant new link in the "Welsh Union" chain was forged in 1895, with the construction of the Wrexham and Ellesmere Railway, which, though an independent Company, with the Hon. George T. Kenyon, M.P., as its first chairman and Mr. O. S. Holt as secretary, was from the outset worked by the Cambrian, and thus formed a new direct connection from that Company's system, into the Denbighshire coal-field, and hence, by the Wrexham, Mold and Connah's Quay, later absorbed by the Great Central, into Chester and the Merseyside.

It was, therefore, no startling departure, when in 1904, the Cambrian sought Parliamentary powers, for which Royal Assent was granted on June 24th, to carry out its previous proposal to amalgamate with the Mid-Wales Railway. This line, some 50 miles in length, which had been constructed about the same time as the Newtown and Llanidloes Railway, and formed a junction with that undertaking at the latter town, had all along been in friendly co-operation with the Cambrian, but the change of company also involved a change of carriages at Llanidloes with consequent delay. From July 1st in that year Cambrian trains began to run through, down the beautiful valley of the Upper Wye, connecting with the Midland system at Three Cocks Junction and then from Talyllyn Junction, over the Brecon and Merthyr Company's metals into Brecon, while on the financial side, stocks and shares of the Mid-Wales were converted into stocks and shares of the Cambrian, and the arrears of interest on the Mid-Wales "B" debenture stock were capitalised into Cambrian "B" debenture stock.

The Mid-Wales like the Cambrian, had had a chequered early career. Indeed, it might be said that its embarrassments began at the cutting of the first sod, when Mr. Whalley, who was as ubiquitous as ever where Welsh railways were concerned, permitted himself to make some remarks, in his speech, disparaging Messrs. David Davies and Savin because he disapproved their method of financing the line. Never before or since has such a scene been witnessed on such an occasion! In vain did some of the influential company present attempt to smooth things over. Mr. Whalley was not to be easily downed, and amidst a chorus of "hisses, whistles and pipes" he was heard declaring that he was a gentleman, a member of

Parliament and a magistrate, and "it was not his place to argue with men like the contractors."

LIEUT.-COL. DAVID DAVIES, M.P.
Chairman 1911-1917.

But that was long ago, and by 1904 had been almost forgotten. What was more present in the public mind was the advantage to owners and traders and travellers alike of the formation of the through route (passing near to the gigantic Birmingham Waterworks at Rhayader, and attaining the highest point on the Cambrian system, at Pantydwr, 947 feet above sea-level), along which, every year, in growing numbers, the Cambrian trains have carried hosts of excursionists from the teeming valleys of South Wales to refresh themselves—and spend money—in the health resorts of Cardigan Bay.

In the same year, too, the Tanat Valley Railway, from Oswestry to Llangynog, to which reference has already been made in a previous chapter, [131] the first sod having been cut at Porthywaen by the Countess of Powis on September 12th, 1899, was opened for traffic. Six years later, in 1910, the Mawddwy Railway, running from Cemmes Road to Dinas Mawddwy, which had formerly belonged to an independent Company and later closed, was re-opened under the Light Railways Act, and worked by the Cambrian, while in 1913, power was obtained to carry out yet another amalgamation, which, small in itself, considerably adds to the amenities of tourist traffic in the neighbourhood of Aberystwyth.

This was the absorption of the little Vale of Rheidol Light Railway, which, authorised by Act of August 6th, 1897, had been constructed on a two feet gauge, with power to enlarge up to 4ft. 8½ inches, from that resort up the valley for just over a dozen miles to the beauteous gorge spanned by the far-famed Devil's Bridge. Though an independent company, its directors were later entirely drawn from the Cambrian Board, with Mr. Alfred Herbert, of Burway, South Croydon, as chairman. The line was opened for goods traffic in August 1902 and for passengers the following December, and since then many thousands of visitors to Aberystwyth have made the delightful journey which its winding course along the hillside affords to lovers of charming scenery. By a subsequent Order, in 1898, an extension of the line was authorised from Aberystwyth to Aberayron, as a separate undertaking with a separate share capital, but this was never attempted, and the Order subsequently expired, in 1904. Under the 1913 amalgamation Scheme the stocks of the Vale of Rheidol Company were converted into Cambrian stock, and the line worked as part of that company's system.

Together with the Welshpool and Llanfair line (already described) [132] which had been opened in 1903, it gave the Cambrian a narrow guage mileage of twenty-one miles, and a total mileage in operation (including the final extension into the commodious new station at Pwllheli in July 1909), of exactly 300 miles, of which twelve only are double line.

II.

But it is not only in length that the Cambrian has developed in recent years. The advance in constructional details and rolling stock is by no means less marked. Following the abolition of second class compartments, in 1912, has come a steady advance in the comfort and convenience of the passenger coaching stock, until to-day, when the latest composite corridor coaches 54 feet long are accepted by other companies for through running. Some of them are regularly worked on through trains, to Manchester, Liverpool, Birmingham and London, and, in the tourist season, to other places in the North of England and South Wales. Recently a dining and luncheon car service has been inaugurated in the summer between Paddington and Aberystwyth, and buffet cars are attached to some of the principal trains between Pwllheli and Aberystwyth and Shrewsbury and Whitchurch all the year round.

During the time when Mr. Herbert Jones, who succeeded the late Mr. Wm. Aston, was locomotive superintendent, [133] a large stride forward was taken in this department. The engines now employed in hauling these long and heavily-ladened tourist trains are mighty monsters compared with what appeared "powerful" enough to travellers in the fifties and sixties. Readers turning to the illustrations on another page may see at a glance the difference between "then" and "now" both in the coaching and the locomotive departments. Even the contrast between the engines as originally constructed and as rebuilt is sufficient to impress the interested traveller, but to these, in late years, have been added a powerful class of passenger and goods engines, weighing, with the tender, 75 tons, the passenger class being bogie engines, with four coupled wheels 6ft. diameter, and the goods being the ordinary six wheel coupled type.

Only one change from the old to the new is, perhaps, regretted by some. One of the qualifications of what is popularly termed the "railwayac,"—the man who, though not in the railway service, is keenly interested in the running and working of trains,—is that he should be able to recite, on demand, an accurate catalogue of engine names. In former days, on the Cambrian, as on some other lines, every engine had its name, and there are still middle-aged men in this locality who carry from boyhood affectionate memory of many of these labels,—the "Albion," the "Milford," the "Mountaineer," the "Plasffynnon," the "Maglona" and "Gladys," the "Glansevern," the "Tubal Cain," the "Prince of Wales" and the like, and, later the "Beaconsfield" and the "Hartington."

To some of the directors, however, the habit of christening engines, especially after distinguished persons or the seats of the local gentry, seemed to savour of flunkeyism and the custom was abandoned. Only on the London and North Western and the Great Western, and the London Brighton and South Coast, the writer believes, does it still generally obtain, and even there it is limited to the larger passenger locomotives. Gone, too, is the old decoration of the tenders with the Prince of Wales's plumes, and the only ornamentation of engines and coaches finally left being the Company's crest, the English rose entwined with the Red Dragon of Wales, the original design for which was made and presented to the directors many years ago by the late Mr. W. W. E. Wynne, of Peniarth, Towyn, a noted antiquarian of his day.

With the increased weight of engines and coaches necessarily came a strengthening of the road. The rebuilding of the old wooden bridges has already been noted, but some of the girder bridges have been rebuilt also, the last of these, over the Severn at Kilkewydd, near Welshpool, having only been completed last year. This is now a fine structure of four clear spans of more than 60 feet, supported by concrete piers and abutments. Then, too, for the light iron rails laid on a sandy ballast of the old days there have been substituted 80 lb. steel rails laid on broken granite ballast, with a corresponding strengthening of the fastenings, sleepers, etc., and to expedite the running of non-stop trains, mainly during the pressure of the tourist season, special appliances have been erected at wayside stations for the exchange of the "tablet," by means of which the working of a single-line railway is controlled, additional passing places have been constructed, station platforms in several cases considerably lengthened, and one or two new stations opened, bringing the total on the system up to 100.

During the war when Park Hall, Oswestry, was converted first into a vast training camp and later, in part, into a German Prisoners of War camp, a large amount of military transport work fell to the Cambrian, a network of sidings being constructed through the area occupied, and about a quarter of a million of troops were carried over the system to and fro, an additional strain on the human and mechanical resources of the Company which, however, was most efficiently sustained.

Nor does this entirely exhaust the efforts of the Company to serve the district through which its railways pass, to increase the comfort and convenience of the travelling public and to augment and proclaim the amenities of the resorts to which it carries us. To this end, two enterprises, though not directly under the control of the Cambrian, but with which they are linked by close co-operative ties, have materially contributed in recent years. Though Mr. Savin's ambitious schemes for erecting hotels to house the tourists whom the trains might bring ended in financial disaster, the idea was an excellent one; and, when revived, some years ago on a more limited scale and under more propitious conditions, it successfully matured in the formation of the Aberystwyth Queen's Hotel Company, of which a prominent Cambrian director, Mr. Alfred Herbert, is chairman, and some other members of the Board, as well as the General Manager, Mr. S. Williamson, are directors, with the Assistant Secretary of the Cambrian, Mr. S. G. Vowles, serving as Secretary. Not the least advantage of this sort of quasi-partnership is the facility which it has enabled the Cambrian to offer to the public in the shape of combined rail and hotel tickets from the principal inland stations on the system, entitling the visitor to travel to and fro and enjoy the excellent week-end hospitality of the Queen's for an inclusive moderate charge.

It may be truly said, however, that no such allurement is required by those who are already familiar with the charms of Cambria as they unfold themselves in almost illimitable variety all along this western seaboard, stretching from the mouth of the Rheidol right up to the lonely fastnesses of Lleyn. It is, therefore, more particularly to the enlightenment of the uninitiated that the Cardigan Bay Resorts Association, of which the Rev. Gwynoro Davies, Barmouth, is chairman and Mr. H. Warwick, superintendent of the Cambrian line (and now its divisional traffic superintendent under the Great Western control), secretary, working in close and sympathetic co-operation, not only with the Cambrian Company, but with several of the local authorities, has done much, year after year, to make known to the potential English tourist the delights which await him on his arrival in these coastal towns.

At any rate the glorious hills and valleys bordering the Bay, which have inspired more than one Welsh literary itinerant to rhapsody, and furnished Mr. Lloyd George with many a homely and figurative peroration, have proved no mean asset to the proprietors of a railway, whose traffic consists so largely of tourists. To the shareholders of the Cambrian has come the satisfaction of knowing that a concern, which was born under, and for many years continued to struggle for its very existence with, the most embarrassing financial conditions, has gradually acquired a more robust economic constitution.

But it has only been accomplished by long and patient conservation of its slender reserves. Mr. Conacher, it used to be said, during his arduous and energetic management, was "improving the Cambrian in the dark." To his successors has been bequeathed the advantage of bringing that quiet sowing to a fruitful and more apparent harvest. Mr. Conacher was succeeded in the secretariat by another wise and diligent officer, the late Mr. Richard Brayne, whose subsequent retirement to a quiet life in the seclusion of the Shropshire village of Kinnerley, was a matter of regret to all who knew and realised his sterling service to the Company.

On the managerial side of the joint-office which Mr. Conacher vacated, following the comparatively short but bustling reign of Mr. Alfred Aslett (during which much was done to redeem the line from an unlucky reputation for unpunctuality that had become locally proverbial), and that of the late Mr. C. S. Denniss, the Company were fortunate in securing for this responsible office, Mr. Samuel Williamson, trained under Mr. Conacher's tutelage, and thus specially fitted to continue that wise and far-seeing policy which had marked his instructor's methods. Under Mr. Williamson's guiding hand, still further assisted in very valuable fashion by Mr. Conacher, when, for a few years before his death, in 1911, he was called to the chair of the Board, and since then by a Board of which Major David Davies, M.P., the grandson of one of the foremost of the Cambrian's pioneers is chairman, the financial position of the Company has very materially improved.

This is reflected in the terms of amalgamation with the Great Western Company. In 1908 the stockholders of the Company received the sum of £96,556, but such was the rapid improvement in the Company's position that in 1913 they received £119,005, that is to say, in the space of five years the amount increased by 23¼ per cent., and it was on this basis that the negotiations with the Great Western Company were carried through in 1922, because for the period from 4th August, 1914, to 15th August, 1921, under the arrangement with the Government, the profits of the Company were fixed on the 1913 basis. Commencing as from 1st January, 1922, the terms of amalgamation give to the proprietors of the Cambrian Company an immediate annual income of £119,307, and this will be increased as from 1st January, 1929, by a further annual sum of £18,161, assuming the dividend on the Ordinary Stock of the Great Western Company remains as at present, viz:—7¼% per annum, thus making a total of £137,468. In addition to this improvement, the Company, on the one hand, during the period from 1909 to 1913, cleared off a heavy debt, and, on the other hand, built up very substantial reserves and, in fact, at the end of 1913, the financial position of the Company was stronger than it had ever been.

Two Faithful Servants.

The late Mr. Richard Brayne,
Secretary 1895-1906.

Mr. T. S. Goldsworthy,
Storekeeper and Senior Officer
of the line at the time of its amalgamation
with the Great Western.

It has, however, been an agency beyond the control of directorate or internal management which has shaped the final destiny of the Company. From time to time during the years up to 1914 rumours have circulated concerning the prospective purchase of the Cambrian by one of its great neighbours, either the Great Western, or, more often, the London and North Western, with which it had long maintained a close working alliance. But nothing ever matured in this direction. Cynics were apt to suggest that the explanation might be sought in the parable of the two dogs and the bone, neither of them really wanting it, but each anxious that the other should not get it. Anyhow, it seemed as if the Cambrian would become permanently established as the largest of the independent Welsh Railways, when the Great War plunged, not only this country, but more than half the civilized world into economic chaos. Emerging from its war-time experience of State-control, the Cambrian, like other railways, found itself faced with a hugely-augmented labour bill, to meet which out of potential future revenue, appeared practically impossible.

It was under these embarrassing circumstances that Sir Eric Geddes, as Minister of Transport, devised his grouping scheme, by which all English, Welsh and Scottish railways are amalgamated in groups as a means to more economical working. Together with all the other independent Welsh Companies, the Cambrian was placed in the Western Group, with the Great Western as absorber, and, the proposal meeting with the approval of the proprietors, to whom the transfer offered, on the whole, a decided financial advantage, while the directors were consoled for loss of office with a grant of £7,000, it was merely left for the Amalgamation Tribunal to give its final assent. This was done early in March and on Lady Day, 1922, almost exactly seventy years after its original inception, the Company, as a separate and independent organisation, officially ceased to be.

III.

Such is the story of the Cambrian. If the reasonable limitations imposed on the prolixity of authorship compel its reduction, in these pages, into more or less broad outline, it is not for lack of plentiful material available to the more meticulous student of its details, out of which, it would be easy to weave a hundred volumes. Lying in the lumber cupboards of solicitors' offices up and down Montgomeryshire, in the strong rooms of Welsh border banks, or amongst the family archives of some of the great country seats of Powysland, there are to be discovered by the diligent searcher masses of old papers, the very existence of which may, perhaps, have been half-forgotten by their present owners, but which waft us back more than half-a-century, and shed varied light on some of the obscurer passages in Welsh railway annals.

Early prospectuses, full of glowing promises of rich dividends the hopes of which have long since become as faded as the now yellow leaves on which they were inscribed. Great tomes of carefully-written-out verbatim notes of Parliamentary Committee evidence. Equally voluminous records of judgments delivered in Chancery by illustrious law-givers long since dead. "Minutes of Orders on Petition," declaring this, that and the other about the safeguarding of certain interests, and the payment of certain dividends—if any funds could be found for the purpose!—and enquiring all sorts of things about "gross receipts" and "monies actually paid into Court, or which shall hereafter be paid into court." Oh, eternal optimism of those early pioneers! Letters from engineers and contractors. Minutes of Board Meetings. Books of accounts of "preliminary expenses," in which "visits to London" seem to bulk so largely and to exhaust so considerable a proportion of the capital subscribed by eager shareholders who believed that some fine day they were to wake to find themselves part owners of a wonderful trunk route yielding illimitable toll upon the wealth of Lancashire and mercantile fleets of the far-reaching seas. They are all there in quaint and often incongruous companionship, and as one turns over their dusty pages and reverently replaces them in their grave of tattered brown paper, one is prompted to reflect, not without a wistful sigh, upon the vanity of human hopes and expectations.

And yet, if the Cambrian never became the great and glorious institution which those pioneers and projectors of its initial component parts intended, and sincerely believed it would, can it be either truly or generously said that their labours were in vain? By their courage and determination and resolute struggle against enormous adversity, they did, at least, bring into being a public service which has opened up remote valleys, formed a link between the great centres of England and of South Wales, and the coast of Cardigan

Bay, and kindled a new life for and offered the opportunity of increased prosperity to many a small country town in Shropshire, Montgomeryshire, and Merioneth. They have created means of employment for thousands of workers, and afforded facilities for recreation for millions more who have thus been enabled and encouraged to spend their holidays amidst the health-giving breezes of the mountains and the sea. And above all they, and their successors in the conduct of the undertaking, with its developing lines, have shown us how, despite the early apathy and even jealousy of neighbouring "giant leviathans," a small independent railway company can faithfully serve its day and generation, until, by one of those unforeseen strokes of irony to which corporate as well as individual life is ever subject, it is thrown by eccentric Fate into the arms of the very Company, under whose protective ægis the originators of the Oswestry and Newtown and the Newtown and Machynlleth Railways so ardently, but vainly, desired to place themselves more than half a century ago.

What may be the outcome of this great change it is yet too early to predict; but, whatever it be, for weal or woe, it is a sad thought to many that what they have so long known, and smiled at, and cursed, and loved as "the poor old Cambrian," officially is no more, and "the debt that cancels all others" is finally discharged.

APPENDIX.

LIST OF CHAIRMEN OF THE CAMBRIAN RAILWAYS SINCE THE CONSOLIDATION OF THE VARIOUS INDEPENDENT UNDERTAKINGS IN 1864.

THE RIGHT HONOURABLE THE EARL VANE. (Afterwards the Most Hon. The Marquess of Londonderry) (1864-1884)

CAPTAIN R. D. PRYCE (1884-1886)

MR. JAMES FREDERIC BUCKLEY (1886-1900)

MR. ARTHUR CHARLES HUMPHREYS-OWEN, M.P. (1900-1905)

MR. WILLIAM BAILEY HAWKINS (1905-1909)

MR. JOHN CONACHER (1909-1911)

LT.-COL. DAVID DAVIES, M.P. (1911-1922)

LIST OF GENERAL MANAGERS SINCE THE DATE OF CONSOLIDATION.

MR. GEORGE LEWIS (1864-1882)

MR. JOHN CONACHER (1890-1891)

MR. ALFRED ASLETT (1891-1895)

MR. C. S. DENNISS (1895-1910)

MR. S. WILLIAMSON (1911-1922)

(Between 1882 and 1890 and again in 1910-11 there was no General Manager, the office being designated traffic manager).

LIST OF SECRETARIES SINCE THE DATE OF CONSOLIDATION.

MR. GEORGE LEWIS (1864-1882)

MR. JOHN CONACHER (1882-1891)

MR. ALFRED ASLETT (1891-1895)

MR. R. BRAYNE (1895-1900)

MR. C. S. DENNISS (1900-1906)

MR. S. WILLIAMSON (1906-1922)

LIST OF DIRECTORS AND OFFICIALS AT THE DATE OF AMALGAMATION, 27th MARCH, 1922.

DIRECTORS—

Chairman: LT.-COL. DAVID DAVIES, M.P., Broneirion, Llandinam, Mont.

Deputy Chairman: THOMAS CRAVEN, ESQ., D.L., J.P., 12a, Kensington Palace Gardens, London, W., 8.

LT.-COL. N. W. APPERLEY, M.V.O., Southend, Durham.

CHARLES BRIDGER ORME CLARKE, ESQ., 4, St. Dunstan's Alley, E.C., 3.

SIR JOSEPH DAVIES, K.B.E., M.P., Dinas Powis, Glam.

ALFRED HERBERT, ESQ., Burway, Harewood Road, South Croydon.

COLONEL RT. HON. LORD KENYON, K.C.V.O., Gredington, Whitchurch, Salop.

THE RT. HON. THE EARL OF POWIS, Powis Castle, Welshpool.

OFFICERS—

Secretary and General Manager: MR. S. WILLIAMSON.

Assistant Secretary: MR. S. G. VOWLES.

Accountant: MR. R. WILLIAMSON.

Engineer and Loco Superintendent: MR. G. C. MCDONALD.

Assistant Engineer: MR. J. WILLIAMSON.

Works Manager: MR. E. COLCLOUGH.

Superintendent of the Line: MR. H. WARWICK.

Goods Manager: MR. W. FINCHETT.

Store Keeper: MR. T. GOLDSWORTHY.

Auditors: MESSRS. JAMES FRASER, 31, Copthall Avenue, E.C.; and CHARLES FOX, 11, Old Jewry Chambers, E.C.

Solicitor: MR. W. KENRICK MINSHALL, Oswestry.

Bankers: LLOYD'S BANK LTD., Oswestry.

SOME OLD TIME TABLES.

1860. OSWESTRY AND NEWTOWN RAILWAY:

UP	1, 2, 3	1, 2, 3	1, 2, 3	1, 2, 3	1, 2, 3	1, 2, 3
WELSHPOOL	6:35	8:45	11:45	2:25	4:05	7:50
Pool Quay	6:50	9:00	12:00	2:40	4:20	8:05
Four Crosses	7:02	9:12	12:12	2:52	4:30	8:17
Llanymynech	7:10	9:20	12:20	3:00	4:40	8:25
Llynclys	7:15	9:25	12:25	3:05	..	8:30
OSWESTRY	7:23	9:35	12:35	3:15	4:55	8:40
DOWN	1, 2, 3	1, 2, 3	1, 2, 3	1, 2, 3	1, 2, 3	1, 2, 3
OSWESTRY	8:20	10:10	1:20	3:45	6:15	9:30
Llynclys	8:28	10:18	1:28	..	6:23	9:38
Llanymynech	8:35	10:25	1:35	3:58	6:30	9:45
Four Crosses	8:43	10:33	1:43	4:07	6:38	9:53
Pool Quay	8:55	10:45	1:55	4:18	6:50	10:05
WELSHPOOL	9:10	11:00	2:10	4:33	7:05	10:20

SUNDAY TRAINS—Trains leave Oswestry (calling at the intermediate Stations) for Welshpool at 10 5 a.m., and 8 0 p.m. Also from Welshpool for Oswestry at 9 0 a.m., and 7 0 p.m.

Omnibuses await the arrival of the trains at Oswestry and Welshpool. An Omnibus will work daily (Sundays excepted) from Llanfyllin, through Llanfechain and Llansaintffraid to Llanymynech, in connection with the 9 20 a.m. up train, and the 6-30 p.m., down train: also between Montgomery and Welshpool in connection with the 8 30 a.m. up train, and the 6 15 p.m. Down Train.

1860. LLANIDLOES AND NEWTOWN RAILWAY.

From Llanidloes STATIONS	1, 2, 3 a.m.	1, 2, P a.m.	1, 2, 3 p.m.	1, 2, 3 p.m.
Llanidloes	6:30	11:00	1:30	7:30
Dolwen	6:38	11:08	1:38	7:38
Llandinam	6:45	11:15	1:45	7:45
Moat Lane	6:53	11:23	1:53	7:53
Newtown	7:05	11:35	2:05	8:05

From Newtown STATIONS	1, 2, P a.m.	1, 2, 3 p.m.	1, 2, 3 p.m.	1, 2, 3 p.m.
Newtown	10:00	12:40	4:00	8:55
Moat Lane	10:12	12:52	4:12	9:07
Llandinam	10:20	1:00	4:20	9:15
Dolwen	10:27	1:07	4:27	9:22
Llanidloes	10:35	1:15	4:35	9:30

1864. AFTER THE LINE WAS OPENED TO ABERYSTWYTH.

(Down Trains).

DOWN									SUNDAYS	
Whitchurch d.			9:35	1:10		4:25	6:15	7:15	9:10	

- 111 -

Fenn's Bank			9:45		4:35		9:20	
Bettisfield			9:52		4:42	6:30	9:27	
Welshampton			9:57		4:47	6:35	9:32	
Ellesmere			10:05	1:36	4:55	6:45	7:40	9:40	
Whittington			10:25	1:50	5:10		9:56	
OSWESTRY a.			10:30	1:55	5:15	7:00	7:55	10:00	
... d.		6:40	10:40	2:05	3:30	5:35	7:05		6:15	5:00
Llynclys		6:50	10:50	2:13	3:40	5:50	7:10		6:25	5:10
Pant			Mon.	W&S		W&S	7:20			
Llanymynech		6:56	10:56	2:20	3:50	6:00			6:31	5:18
Four Crosses		7:00	10:00		3:55	6:07	7:27		6:35	5:24
Arddleen		146a	Mon.	W&S		W&S				
Pool Quay		7:09	10:10		4:05	6:20			6:44	5:35

Buttington			7:15	10:20	2:35	4:10	6:30	7:47		6:50	5:39
WELSHPOOL a.			7:20	10:25	2:40	4:15	6:40	7:52		6:55	5:45
. . . d.			7:30	10:35	2:50		6:55	7:55		7:05	5:50
Forden			7:40	10:45			7:10			7:17	6:02
Montgomery			7:45	10:50	3:05		7:20	8:15		7:25	6:10
Abermule			7:55	12:00			7:30			7:35	6:20
NEWTOWN		6:10	8:08	12:10	3:25		7:40	8:30		7:48	6:33
Scafell			8:14				7:45				6:40
Moat Lane Junct. a.		6:25	8:22	12:25	3:35		7:50			8:03	6:45
. . . d.		6:30	8:25	12:30	3:35			8:40		8:10	
. . . Moat Lane Junct.			8:25	12:28	3:39		7:52	8:45		8:05	6:48
. . . Llandinam			8:29		3:47		8:00	8:51		8:09	7:00

. . . Dolwen			8:36		3:55		8:08	9:00		8:18	7:07
. . . LLANIDLOES			8:45	12:40			8:16	9:10		8:25	7:15
Caersws		6:38		12:35	146b			8:44		8:14	
Pontdolgoch				12:45				[146b]		8:21	
Carno		7:15		12:58				8:57		8:35	
Llanbrynmair		7:50		1:18	4:15			9:17		8:55	
Cemmes Road		8:10		1:35	4:30			9:32		9:10	
MACHYNLLETH		8:35		2:00	4:45			9:45		9:25	
Glan-Dovey		8:50		2:12	5:00					9:40	
Ynys Las		9:15		2:27	5:15					10:00	
. . . Ynyslas (by ferry)		9:31		2:34	5:20						
. . . Aberdovey	7:25	10:00		3:00	6:00						
. . .	7:	10:		3:1	6:1						

- 114 -

Towyn	37	12		2	0					
... Llwyngwril	a.	10:30		3:30	6:30					
Borth arr.		9:25		2:32	5:20		10:10		10:05	
Llanfihangel		9:30		2:40	5:30				10:13	
Bow Street		9:40		2:47	5:45		10:20		10:20	
Aberystwyth		10:00		3:00	5:55		10:30		10:35	

1864. AFTER THE LINE WAS OPENED TO ABERYSTWYTH.

(Up Trains).

UP	a.m.	a.m.	a.m.	a.m.	p.m.	p.m.	p.m.	SUNDAYS	a.m.	p.m.
Aberystwyth			8:00		1:00		5:30			5:30
Bow Street			8:15		1:13		5:45			5:45
Llanfihangel			8:22				5:52			5:52
Borth			8:30		1:25		6:00			6:00
... Llwyngwril					12:15		4:10			4:10

- 115 -

. . . Towyn			7:45		12:35		4:30		4:30
. . . Aberdovey			7:55		12:45		4:40		4:40
. . . Ynys-las (by ferry) a.			8:25		1:20		5:10		5:10
Ynys-Las			8:35		1:30		6:05		6:05
Glan-Dovey			8:50				6:20		6:20
MACHYNLLETH			9:05		2:00		6:30		6:30
Cemmes Road			9:20		2:15		6:45		6:45
Llanbrynmair			9:35		2:30		7:00		7:00
Carno			9:55		2:50		7:20		7:20
Pontdolgoch			10:07		2:50				
Caersws			10:13				7:40		7:40
. . . LLANIDLOES	6:00		10:00		2:50	5:30	7:20	7:30	8:30	7:20
. . . Dolwen	6:0		10:			5:3	7:2	7:36		7:2

	6		06		6	6			6
. . . Llandinam	6:14		10:14		3:02	5:43	7:34	7:44		7:34
. . . Moat Lane Junc.	6:22		10:20		3:10	5:50	7:42	7:55		7:42
Moat Lane Junc. a.			10:16		3:10		7:45			7:45
. . . d.			10:26		3:15	6:00	7:50			7:50
Scafell	6:29					6:05				
NEWTOWN	6:34		10:35		3:25	6:15	8:00		8:55	8:00
Abermule	6:45		10:45			6:25	8:07		9:00	8:07
Montgomery	6:55		10:55		3:45	6:35	8:17		9:08	8:17
Forden	7:00	[147a]	11:02			6:41				
WELSHPOOL a.	7:12		11:15		4:00	6:55	8:35		9:27	8:35
. . . d.	7:16	9:00	11:25		4:10	7:00	8:45		9:35	8:45
Buttington	7:21	9:05	11:31		4:15	7:05	8:51		9:40	8:51
Pool Quay	7:2	9:15	11:		4:19	7:1	8:5		9:4	8:5

	8		38			3	7		6	7
Arddleen	W&S	9:20	W&S		Mon.					
Four Crosses	7:40	9:30	11:50		4:29	7:22	9:06		9:55	9:06
Llanymynech	7:46	9:35	12:00		4:35	7:27	9:12		10:01	9:12
Pant	W&S	9:40	W&S		Mon.					
Llynclys	7:56	9:50	12:10	1 & 2	4:45	7:38	9:20		10:10	9:20
OSWESTRY a.	8:05	10:00	12:20	p.m.	4:55 [147 b]	7:50	9:30		10:20	9:30
. . . d.	8:10	11:20	12:25	2:10	5:15	7:55				
Whittington	8:14	11:25		2:14	5:19	8:00				
Ellesmere	8:27	11:41	12:40	2:30	5:35	8:15				
Welshampton	8:32	11:50		2:38	5:43	8:25				

Bettisfield	8:37	11:55		2:42	5:47	8:30
Fenn's Bank	8:46	12:02		2:49	5:54	8:37
Whitchurch	8:54	12:12	1:00	3:00	6:05	8:50